OPPOSING VIEWPOINTS® SERIES

D0499320

Human Genetics

Other Books of Related Interest:

Opposing Viewpoints Series
Birth Defects

Genetic Engineering

Human Rights

At Issue Series
Are Abortion Rights Threatened?

Designer Babies

Has Child Behavior Worsened?

Current Controversies Series
Medical Ethics

"Congress shall make no law . . . abridging the freedom of speech, or of the press."

First Amendment to the US Constitution

The basic foundation of our democracy is the First Amendment guarantee of freedom of expression. The Opposing Viewpoints Series is dedicated to the concept of this basic freedom and the idea that it is more important to practice it than to enshrine it.

I Human Genetics

Louise I. Gerdes, Book Editor

GREENHAVEN PRESS
A part of Gale, Cengage Learning

GALE
CENGAGE Learning·

Farmington Hills, Mich • San Francisco • New York • Waterville, Maine
Meriden, Conn • Mason, Ohio • Chicago

GALE
CENGAGE Learning·

Elizabeth Des Chenes, *Director, Content Strategy*
Douglas Dentino, *Manager, New Product*

For more information, contact:
Greenhaven Press
27500 Drake Rd.
Farmington Hills, MI 48331-3535
Or you can visit our Internet site at gale.cengage.com

For product information and technology assistance, contact us at

Gale Customer Support, 1-800-877-4253
For permission to use material from this text or product, submit all requests online at www.cengage.com/permissions

Further permissions questions can be emailed to permissionrequest@cengage.com

Articles in Greenhaven Press anthologies are often edited for length to meet page requirements. In addition, original titles of these works are changed to clearly present the main thesis and to explicitly indicate the author's opinion. Every effort is made to ensure that Greenhaven Press accurately reflects the original intent of the authors. Every effort has been made to trace the owners of copyrighted material.

Cover image copyright © Chepko Danil Vitalevich/Shutterstock.com.

LIBRARY OF CONGRESS CATALOGING-IN-PUBLICATION DATA

Human genetics / Louise I. Gerdes, book editor.
　　p. cm. -- (Opposing viewpoints)
　　Includes bibliographical references and index.
　　Summary: "Opposing Viewpoints is the leading source for libraries and class-rooms in need of current-issue materials. The viewpoints are selected from a wide range of highly respected sources and publications"-- Provided by publisher.
　　ISBN 978-0-7377-6953-1 (hardback) -- ISBN 978-0-7377-6954-8 (paperback)
　　1. Genes--Juvenile literature. 2. Human genetics--Juvenile literature. I. Gerdes, Louise I., 1953- editor of compilation.
　　QH447.H834 2014
　　572.8'6--dc23
　　　　　　　　　　　　　　　　　　　　　　　　　　　　　2014002607

Printed in the United States of America
1 2 3 4 5 6 7 18 17 16 15 14

Contents

Chapter 4: What Is the Impact of Collecting Human Genetic Information?

Why Consider Opposing Viewpoints?

> *"The only way in which a human being can make some approach to knowing the whole of a subject is by hearing what can be said about it by persons of every variety of opinion and studying all modes in which it can be looked at by every character of mind. No wise man ever acquired his wisdom in any mode but this."*
>
> *John Stuart Mill*

In our media-intensive culture it is not difficult to find differing opinions. Thousands of newspapers and magazines and dozens of radio and television talk shows resound with differing points of view. The difficulty lies in deciding which opinion to agree with and which "experts" seem the most credible. The more inundated we become with differing opinions and claims, the more essential it is to hone critical reading and thinking skills to evaluate these ideas. Opposing Viewpoints books address this problem directly by presenting stimulating debates that can be used to enhance and teach these skills. The varied opinions contained in each book examine many different aspects of a single issue. While examining these conveniently edited opposing views, readers can develop critical thinking skills such as the ability to compare and contrast authors' credibility, facts, argumentation styles, use of persuasive techniques, and other stylistic tools. In short, the Opposing Viewpoints Series is an ideal way to attain the higher-level thinking and reading skills so essential in a culture of diverse and contradictory opinions.

In addition to providing a tool for critical thinking, Opposing Viewpoints books challenge readers to question their own strongly held opinions and assumptions. Most people form their opinions on the basis of upbringing, peer pressure, and personal, cultural, or professional bias. By reading carefully balanced opposing views, readers must directly confront new ideas as well as the opinions of those with whom they disagree. This is not to argue simplistically that everyone who reads opposing views will—or should—change his or her opinion. Instead, the series enhances readers' understanding of their own views by encouraging confrontation with opposing ideas. Careful examination of others' views can lead to the readers' understanding of the logical inconsistencies in their own opinions, perspective on why they hold an opinion, and the consideration of the possibility that their opinion requires further evaluation.

Evaluating Other Opinions

To ensure that this type of examination occurs, Opposing Viewpoints books present all types of opinions. Prominent spokespeople on different sides of each issue as well as well-known professionals from many disciplines challenge the reader. An additional goal of the series is to provide a forum for other, less known, or even unpopular viewpoints. The opinion of an ordinary person who has had to make the decision to cut off life support from a terminally ill relative, for example, may be just as valuable and provide just as much insight as a medical ethicist's professional opinion. The editors have two additional purposes in including these less known views. One, the editors encourage readers to respect others' opinions—even when not enhanced by professional credibility. It is only by reading or listening to and objectively evaluating others' ideas that one can determine whether they are worthy of consideration. Two, the inclusion of such viewpoints encourages the important critical thinking skill of objectively evaluating an author's credentials and bias. This evaluation will illuminate an author's reasons for taking a particular stance on an issue and will aid in readers' evaluation of the author's ideas.

It is our hope that these books will give readers a deeper understanding of the issues debated and an appreciation of the complexity of even seemingly simple issues when good and honest people disagree. This awareness is particularly important in a democratic society such as ours in which people enter into public debate to determine the common good. Those with whom one disagrees should not be regarded as enemies but rather as people whose views deserve careful examination and may shed light on one's own.

Thomas Jefferson once said that "difference of opinion leads to inquiry, and inquiry to truth." Jefferson, a broadly educated man, argued that "if a nation expects to be ignorant and free . . . it expects what never was and never will be." As individuals and as a nation, it is imperative that we consider the opinions of others and examine them with skill and discernment. The Opposing Viewpoints Series is intended to help readers achieve this goal.

David L. Bender and Bruno Leone,
Founders

Introduction

"Genetic engineers represent our fondest hopes and aspirations as well as our darkest fears and misgivings. That's why most discussions of the new technology are likely to be so heated. The technology touches the core of our self-definition."

Jeremy Rifkin,
economic and social theorist and
political activist, The Biotech Century

Although the science of human genetics is difficult for most to understand, the social implications of its use impact all humanity. Policy makers, most of whom are not familiar with the complexities of genetic science, must make significant decisions about the use of human genetic technology. Public opinion, which often informs policy, further complicates the process, as people's opinions about issues related to human genetics are rarely based on only the science; they are instead influenced by the views of others such as bioethicists, philosophers, and storytellers. Indeed, these divergent views reflect the overarching human genetics debate. One question explored from these varying perspectives is the potential impact of human genetic enhancement, the manipulation of genes to achieve a variety of ends from curing genetic diseases to selecting a child's physical and intellectual characteristics.

One influential point of view about human genetic enhancements comes from popular culture. Popular culture has a significant influence on how the general public views science. In fact, research reveals that those who habitually consume popular culture have a more negative attitude toward science than those who do not. According to David A. Kirby, a genetics and molecular biology professor who explores the impact of media on science, "The effect of popular culture on public conceptions of science is also compounded by the fact that much of the public's exposures to science is through fictional representations."[1] One of the fictional narratives that Kirby finds particularly influential on public opinion about human genetic enhancement is the film *Gattaca* (1997), produced by Sony Pictures and written and directed by Andrew Niccol. The film derives its title from a combination of the first letters of the four bases of DNA: guanine, adenine, thymine, and cytosine.

Gattaca's filmmaker portrays a dystopian future in which parents are able to select the genetic traits of their children. One son, Vincent Freeman, the film's protagonist, is genetically unenhanced. However, Anton, his younger brother; Irene, his love interest; and Eugene, the man whose genetic profile Vincent borrows, are all genetically enhanced. Vincent borrows the genetic profile so he can work as an engineer and achieve his dream of becoming an astronaut. Although genetic discrimination is illegal in the world of *Gattaca*, the reality is that the people in the film's world refer to those who are not genetically enhanced in derogatory terms such as "faith births," "in-valids," and "de-gene-erates." In the words of Vincent, "We now have discrimination down to a science."

Indeed, some genetic scientists share the filmmaker's fears that genetic enhancement will lead to genetic discrimination. Evolutionary geneticist Richard Lewontin, for example, believes that "a large fraction of human beings will be the victims of the omissions and commissions of science because they lack the material wealth and the social power to control their own lives."[2] Molecular biologist Lee Silver agrees, main-

---

1. David A. Kirby, "The New Eugenics in Cinema: Genetic Determinism and Gene Therapy in *Gattaca*," *Science Fiction Studies*, July 2000.
2. Quoted in Kirby, *op. cit.*

taining that this will lead to a society of genetic haves and have-nots. "That's my fear about genetic engineering: it is so powerful, it is so good, it will only be available to those who have money."[3]

In the film, however, Vincent actually proves to be a superior human being despite his lack of enhancement. He excels physically and socially despite his built-in flaws. In truth, his defects have provided him with a trait that the genetically enhanced characters do not posses—inner strength. Indeed, says Kirby, in the world of *Gattaca*, "The price paid for a genetically perfect world is the loss of the 'human spirit.'"

Several scenes symbolically reflect Vincent's spirit. In one instance, the myopic Vincent removes his contact lenses to escape detection by police. He is virtually blind, but crosses a busy highway to keep his date with his love interest, Irene. He saves his brother Anton from drowning, although he has many physical defects that his younger brother does not have. Thus, unlike some science fiction genetic engineering narratives, in the eyes of Kirby, the film was less about the perils of science and more about the dangers of genetic determinism. "*Gattaca* does not deny the importance of genes, nor does it fault the technology itself; rather, the film warns of the problems that arise if we believe that humans are nothing more than their genes."

Gattaca also examines one other potentially unintended consequence of human genetic enhancement—the loss of diversity. The movie suggests that diversity is lost in a world that narrowly defines what is normal and where people are genetically enhanced to meet increasingly narrow social norms. The world of *Gattaca* is dull, colorless, and antiseptic. The sets developed by Jan Roelfs are sterile, with smooth, stainless steel surfaces. All of the employees of the company, men and women alike, wear matching black suits. Some bioethicists share this fear that in a world with little diversity, much of

3. Quoted in Kirby, *op. cit.*

what makes us human will be lost. Bioethicist Leon Kass, author of *Life, Liberty, and the Defense of Dignity: The Challenge for Bioethics*, argues that technical mastery over human nature will inevitably lead to dehumanization:

> Homogenization, mediocrity, pacification, drug-induced contentment, debasement of taste, souls without loves and longings—these are the inevitable results of making the essence of human nature the last project of technical mastery. In his moment of triumph, Promethean man will become a contented cow.

This dystopic image of humanity is in many ways eerily similar to the world of *Gattaca*.

To limit the impact of these dystopian visions, some analysts recommend regulations or even bans of genetic enhancement. Francis Fukuyama, professor of international political economy at Johns Hopkins University and author of *Our Posthuman Future: Consequences of the Biotechnology Revolution*, recommends regulation so that human genetic science progresses slowly and cautiously. Fukuyama claims that people will pass genetic modifications to future generations and the safety concerns will thus multiply. Indeed, as Fukuyama suggests, genetic causation is complex—many genes can interact to create one outcome, and single genes can have many effects. "When a long-term genetic effect may not show up for decades after the procedure is administered, parents will risk a multitude of unintended and largely irreversible consequences for their children. This would seem to be a situation calling for strict regulation," he wrote in a 2000 article for *Reason*. In response to claims that regulation threatens valuable innovation and personal freedom, Fukuyama argues that bioethicists and policy makers have long recognized the need to slow science. "We slow the progress of science today for all sorts of ethical reasons. Biomedicine could advance much faster if we abolished our rules on human experimentation in clinical trials, as Nazi researchers did." Indeed, governments worldwide regulate biomedical technology in a variety of ways. "I don't think that a set of regulations designed to focus future bio-medicine on therapeutic rather than enhancement purposes constitutes oppressive state intervention," Fukuyama wrote.

Some bioethicists, however, disagree. Bioethicist Gregory Stock, director of the Program of Medicine, Technology, and Society at the University of California, Los Angeles School of Medicine and author of *Redesigning Humans: Our Inevitable Genetic Future*, claims that Fukuyama's regulatory recommen-dations will, in fact, threaten scientific advancement and free-dom of choice. Stock fears that regulations and bans will drive research underground. Moreover, he argues, since prohibitions have not stopped people from accessing harmful substances such as alcohol and dangerous drugs, biomedical technology bans are not likely to prevent people from using these tech-nologies. Indeed, vague, unsubstantiated fears will not prevent human enhancement, he asserts. "As we decipher our biology and learn to modify it, we are learning to modify ourselves—and we will do so. No laws will stop this," he wrote for *Reason* in 2000. Stock does agree that genetic enhancement technol-ogy will force people to question what it means to be a hu-man being, but he still contends: "However uneasy these new technologies make us, if we wish to continue to lead the way in shaping the human future we must actively explore them."

Not unlike Stock and like-minded bioethicists, transhu-manist philosophers believe that human enhancement tech-nology should be widely available and that people, not gov-ernments, should decide which technologies they will use. They maintain that the so-called posthuman future need not be dystopian. Nick Bostrom, a Swedish-born philosopher who is the director of the Future of Humanity Institute at Oxford University, argues that transhumanism is simply a further de-velopment of what began during the Enlightenment. Also known as the Age of Reason, the Enlightenment was a period that began at the end of the seventeenth century, during which intellectuals emphasized reason and individualism and the advancement of knowledge through the scientific method—while also challenging ideas grounded in tradition and faith. Since the beginning of the Enlightenment, science has led to significant improvements in the human condition. According to Bostrom, humans can continue to improve through the use of applied science and other rational methods, making it possible to increase the human life span and extend intellectual and physical capacities.

Transhumanists dispute claims like those of Kass that genetic technology threatens human dignity. Bostrom suggests that humankind's nature need not be held up as an ideal standard when humankind's inhumanity is well documented. Indeed, he argues, conserving the current status of human dignity is limiting. In a 2005 article in *Bioethics*, Bostrom maintains, "The set of individuals accorded full moral status by Western societies has actually increased [over the years] to include men without property or noble descent, women, and non-white peoples. It would seem feasible to extend this set further to include future posthumans." Transhumanists believe that human dignity is not found in human genes but in what humans have the potential to become. Indeed, Bostrom notes, "In the eyes of a hunter-gatherer, we might already appear 'posthuman.' Yet these radical extensions of human capabilities—some of them biological, others external—have not divested us of moral status or dehumanized us in the sense of making us generally unworthy and base." Indeed, he asserts, by defending posthuman dignity we embrace more inclusive and humane ethics.

Clearly, philosophers, bioethicists, and filmmakers as well as genetic, biomedical, and political scientists envision different human genetic enhancement futures. Whether dystopian or bright, these visions inform public opinion and, in turn, how policy makers will respond to human genetic enhancement technologies and other policy challenges facing human genomic science. The authors of the viewpoints in *Opposing Viewpoints: Human Genetics* explore these issues in the following chapters: Should People Embrace Human Genetic Enhancements and Therapies?, Should Biotech Companies Be Allowed to Patent Human Genes?, Are Human Genetic Tests Beneficial?, and What Is the Impact of Collecting Human Genetic Information? The answers to these questions, some argue, will have a significant impact on the future of humanity. According to Bostrom and fellow Oxford University philosopher and bioethicist Julian Savulescu in *Human Advancement*, advances in technology, including human genetic technology, "will provide the opportunity fundamentally to change the human condition. This presents both great risks and enormous potential benefits. Our fate is, to a greater degree than ever before in human history, in our own hands."

OPPOSING
VIEWPOINTS®
SERIES

Should People Embrace Human Genetic Enhancements and Therapies?

Chapter Preface

One of several claimed benefits of advances in human genetic knowledge is pharmacogenomics—the study of how genetic makeup influences a person's response to drugs. Genetic science has revealed that genes encode enzymes that influence how people metabolize prescription drugs. The goal of pharmacogenomics is to optimize the impact of drug therapies while minimizing the adverse effects based on the patient's genotype. For example, research shows that people with certain genetic profiles break down drugs too quickly, which can cause negative side effects. According to genetics professor James P. Evans, "The poster child for pharmacogenomics is the HIV/AIDS drug Abacavir." Researchers discovered that HIV-infected patients with a particular genetic variant had a negative reaction to the drug Abacavir. Thus, doctors now routinely test HIV-infected patients for this genetic variant. This discovery was a significant breakthrough in HIV treatment and unearthed the potential value of pharmacogenomics.

The study of the connection between genes and drugs also revealed that some patients with a unique genetic profile do not metabolize drugs quickly, thus weakening the therapeutic value of these drugs. Genetic tests can now help doctors determine the appropriate dosage for these patients. As a result, over 120 drugs approved by the US Food and Drug Administration include pharmacogenomic information on their labels. This genetically personalized medicine has stirred debate over whether people should embrace human genetic enhancements and therapies. Some see great health care promise in pharmacogenomics while others believe that the complexities of the human genome and its interconnection with lifestyle choices make the value of pharmacogenomics unrealistic.

Some advocates of pharmacogenomics cite the high cost of adverse drug reactions. According to Dr. Kathryn Teng, director of the Center for Personalized Healthcare at the Cleveland Clinic, an Ohio research hospital, adverse drug reactions are a leading cause of death in hospital patients. Nevertheless, she claims, "Our current practice of prescribing for adult patients is largely trial-and-error, with the same dose given to all patients." Teng believes that pharmacogenomics can improve patient care through personalization. She recognizes that encouraging the use of pharmacogenomics will require more studies that better determine its efficacy. Moreover, helping primary care physicians keep up with the latest research will be essential. "Given the breadth of diseases treated and drugs prescribed by primary care physicians, it is unrealistic for most to keep track of the vast body of literature of pharmacogenomic testing and to decipher how to apply this to clinical practice," she concludes.

Other advocates of pharmacogenomics cite success in personalizing the treatment of disease. For example, research revealed that the breast cancer drug Herceptin was effective for only one in five women. These women had a mutation in their tumor cells that distinguished them from those breast cancer patients who did not respond to the drug. Thus, Genetech, the California biotech company that developed the drug, also sold a diagnostic test that determined who would benefit. However, even in the eyes of advocates, pharmacogenomic science is in its infancy and discoveries that produce tangible results are slow in coming. According to Heino von Prondynski, CEO of the Swiss gene-based diagnostic company, Roche Diagnostics, "Herceptin, I believe, was just a lucky punch."

Other analysts are more cautious. Identifying which genes impact which drugs is a complex and challenging research problem. Researchers must identify and analyze millions of proteins on the 3-billion-base human genome to determine their impact on drug response. According to some commentators in the *Journal of Clinical Medical Research,* "Since many genes are likely to influence responses, obtaining the big picture on the impact of gene variations is highly time-consuming and complicated." Moreover, they assert, if patients have a particular condition and their genetic makeup prevents them from using certain drugs, they are left without alternatives. "Most pharmaceutical companies have been successful with their 'one size fits all' approach to drug development. Since it costs hundreds of millions of dollars to bring a drug to market, will these companies be willing to develop alternative drugs that serve only a small portion of the population?" Indeed, some question how drug companies will proceed in the age of genetically personalized medicine.

Whether or not pharmacogenomics will revolutionize personalized medicine remains controversial. The authors in the following chapter present their views in other controversies surrounding the question of whether people should embrace human genetic enhancements and therapies. Dr. Teng concludes: "Regardless of our personal feelings about the clinical usefulness of genetic testing . . . we need to work together to determine clinical utility and validity and to develop efficient ways to put into practice findings that could affect patient care."

"There are signs that patients might soon start benefiting from gene therapies."

Gene Therapies Have the Potential to Improve Human Health

Scott Kirsner

Despite setbacks, biotechnology companies are pursuing gene therapies that show signs of promise as cures for debilitating genetic diseases, says Boston Globe *correspondent Scott Kirsner in the following viewpoint. Gene therapies create factories using disarmed viruses that, when installed in the body, produce a missing enzyme or protein, and primate studies show that they work. For example, one promising gene therapy produces a protein that helps children with deadly cerebral adrenoleukodystrophy while another creates an enzyme lacking in those with Parkinson's disease. Indeed, investors are once again showing interest in gene therapies, Kirsner concludes.*

As you read, consider the following questions:

1. According to Kirsner, why did gene therapies that seemed to be just over the horizon in the 1990s keep receding?

2. With what have the disarmed viruses of gene therapy factories been packed, in the author's view?

3. In Sam Wadsworth's opinion, how long may the gene factories that help Parkinson's patients last?

A lan Smith can still recall his excitement, in the early 1990s, over early experiments in lab rats that demonstrated gene therapy's potential power to attack diseases such as cystic fibrosis.

Slow, Quiet Progress

Smith, a former chief scientific officer at Genzyme, the Cambridge biotech company, remembers feeling like the experiments were "steppingstones" to developing a whole new wave of medicines for untreatable diseases. Often, they were touted in Genzyme's annual reports, and the research was funded with tens of millions of dollars from stock market investors.

But more than two decades later, there is still no gene therapy that has won approval from the US Food and Drug Administration [FDA], and Genzyme gave up on it as a potential approach to treating cystic fibrosis. What seemed in the 1990s to be a new world just over the horizon kept receding. There were years of "slow, quiet progress," in Smith's words, but also setbacks, including deaths and complications for patients who enrolled in early trials.

In 2013, though, there are signs that patients might soon start benefiting from gene therapies. A Cambridge company, Bluebird Bio, last month [May 2013] filed to sell stock to the public; it hopes to raise $86 million to bring to market a gene therapy that would treat a rare, fatal neurodegenerative disease known as CCALD. (Bluebird's roots go back to 1992, when it was founded as Genetix Pharmaceuticals.)

A Dutch company, uniQure BV, is working to set up a production facility in the Boston area that could eventually employ 50 or more people, according to Philip Astley-Sparke, president of uniQure's new US division. In November [2012], the company received regulatory approval in Europe for a gene therapy called Glybera, which treats patients with a rare metabolic disorder that causes inflammation of the pancreas. It's the first gene therapy to receive regulatory approval anywhere in the Western world—though not yet from the FDA.

Creating Microscopic Factories

How exactly do these new therapies work? Instead of a pill or an injection to treat a chronic ailment, many of the gene therapy approaches essentially try to install a microscopic factory inside your body. Its job is to crank out a missing enzyme or therapeutic protein continually, over the course of years. Studies in primates have seen these factories operate for more than a decade.

The factories themselves are created by using disarmed viruses—the same ones that might ordinarily give you the flu—that have been packed with custom-crafted DNA or RNA. They infiltrate cells in your body and tell them exactly what to make. (The use of viruses for good, not evil, dates back to the late 1700s, when scientists discovered how to inoculate people against smallpox.) These viruses can be delivered to the body by injection or inhalation, or by removing cells from the patient, exposing them to the virus, and reintroducing them to the patient.

Bluebird takes that last approach with a product it is developing for childhood cerebral adrenoleukodystrophy, a disease that affects boys between the ages of 4 and 10, usually leading to a vegetative state and death. (It was featured in the movie "Lorenzo's Oil.") UniQure's product, Glybera, is delivered via a one-time set of injections to the leg. In this case, the factory is making a protein that helps the body break down fats. Without it, the pancreas becomes inflamed, which is painful and in some cases fatal.

How Gene Therapy Works

For many viruses, researchers can disarm the genes responsible for the damaging properties and replace them with genetic instructions to make therapeutic proteins. These viruses that have been redesigned by researchers are called vectors. They are a means to smuggle therapeutic genes into the body.

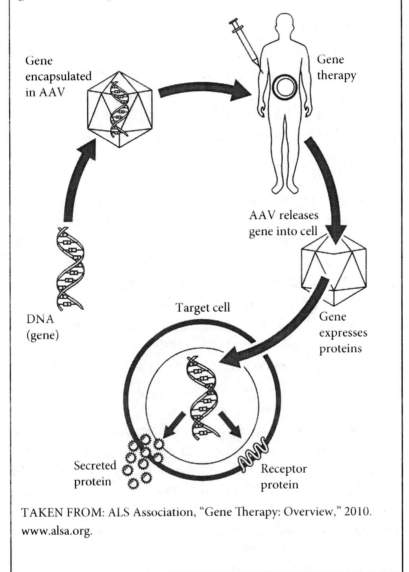

Gene encapsulated in AAV

Gene therapy

AAV releases gene into cell

DNA (gene)

Target cell

Gene expresses proteins

Secreted protein

Receptor protein

TAKEN FROM: ALS Association, "Gene Therapy: Overview," 2010. www.alsa.org.

Somewhere between 1,000 and 5,000 people in the world have the disease Glybera targets, called lipoprotein lipase deficiency. Given that small patient population, uniQure's treatment will set a record for drug prices: about $1.6 million per patient. It is expected to be on the market this year. But uniQure's local facility probably won't produce Glybera, according to Astley-Sparke. It will make future gene therapy products for the company, targeting diseases like hemophilia. "We hope to have it up and running around 2015," he says.

A Stubborn Pursuit

Other companies are focusing on diseases that affect larger patient populations.

Genzyme, now a part of the French pharmaceutical giant Sanofi SA, never abandoned its research into gene therapy. Sam Wadsworth, head of gene therapy research and development, arrived at the company in 1993. Since then, "we have been consistently and persistently and stubbornly pursuing this," he says.

The company is working on a treatment for age-related macular degeneration, a common cause of blindness in people over 50, and for Parkinson's, a neurodegenerative disease. Between 7 million and 10 million people worldwide suffer from Parkinson's according to the Parkinson's Disease Foundation, a patient advocacy group.

In Parkinson's, Wadsworth says, there is already evidence that the gene treatment may have an effect for as long as five years, helping supply an enzyme lacking in those who have Parkinson's and allowing them to stay on lower doses of a drug they use called Levodopa. In macular degeneration, Genzyme's clinical trial is still recruiting patients; some will be treated locally, at Ophthalmic Consultants of Boston.

A Tufts University School of Medicine spin-out, Hemera Biosciences, raised $3.75 million earlier this year, an amount it hopes to use to start clinical trials of a gene therapy treatment for age-related macular degeneration.

In March, the investment bank Lazard Capital Markets published a research report optimistically titled "Gene Therapy: The Time is Now." It cited uniQure's approval in Europe as a major turning point for the approach. And last fall, Smith attended a meeting of investors at the Royal Society in London, where the consensus was that gene therapy, more than 20 years after his early research at Genzyme, is now a promising place to deploy capital.

"I remain excited," says Smith, now semiretired and living in Wayland [Massachusetts]. "Eventually, this will crack. There's no doubt."

*"Overselling the benefits of personal ge-
nomics can hurt the science, by creating unrealistic expectations, and distract us from other, more effective areas
of health promotion."*

Focusing on Human Genomics to Improve Human Health Is Impractical

Timothy Caulfield

*Exaggerated claims that human genetic information will revolu-
tionize health care do more harm than good, argues Timothy
Caulfield in the following viewpoint. He says the gene-disease
connection is complex and, in many cases, knowing one's genetic
makeup has little predictive value. Moreover, tailored genetic
therapies are distant. Regrettably, Caulfield maintains, studies
show that few people change their lifestyle based on genetic information and that living a healthy lifestyle is more likely to improve personal health than knowing one's genome sequence.
Caulfield, Canada Research Chair in Health, Law and Policy at
the University of Alberta, is author of* The Cure for Everything:
Untangling the Twisted Messages About Health, Fitness, and
Happiness.

As you read, consider the following questions:

1. In Caulfield's view, how much will it soon cost to get a copy of one's own genome sequence?

2. What did the ENCODE project reveal about the human genome, according to Caulfield?

3. According to the study Caufield cites concerning depression drugs, how many of the 500,000 genetic markers predicted treatment outcome?

In the very near future, we'll all be able to have our entire genome—all our genetic information—mapped for under $1,000. This is an astonishing scientific development. The Human Genome Project cost billions. Soon, you'll be able to get your very own genome sequenced for the price of a laptop.

It has been suggested that this technological advance will usher in a new health-care "revolution." It will allow us, or so it's promised, to individualize health-care treatments and preventive strategies—an approach often called "personalized medicine." It will allow us to become fully aware of our genetic shortcomings and the diseases for which we're at increased genetic risk, thus providing the impetuous to adopt healthier lifestyles.

An Unlikely Revolution

But will having your personal genome available really revolutionize your health-care world? Will you be able to use this information to significantly improve your chances of avoiding the most common chronic diseases? Not likely.

Tangible benefits will be (and have been) achieved. But, for the most part, these advances are likely to be incremental in nature—which, history tells us, is the way scientific progress usually unfolds.

Why this "we are not in a revolution" message? Overselling the benefits of personal genomics can hurt the science, by creating unrealistic expectations, and distract us from other, more effective areas of health promotion.

The relationship between our genome and disease is far more complicated than originally anticipated. Indeed, the more we learn about the human genome, the less we seem to know. For example, results from a major international initiative to explore all the elements of our genome (the ENCODE project) found that, despite decades-old conventional wisdom that much of our genome was nothing but "junk DNA," as much as 80 per cent of our genome likely has some biological function. This work hints that things are much more convoluted than expected. So much so that one of ENCODE's lead researchers, Yale's Mark Gerstein [bioinformatics scientist], was quoted as saying that it's "like opening a wire closet and seeing a hairball of wires."

Little Predictive Value

Given this complexity, it's no surprise that the personal health value of genomic information, particularly in relation to common diseases, remains questionable. Beyond the comparatively rare single-gene diseases (Huntington's, cystic fibrosis, etc.) and a handful of relatively predictive cancer genes, the kind of genetic information you get from a personal genome scan simply isn't that predictive, especially when compared with the prognostic tools we already have—such as the weigh scale, tape measure and blood pressure cuff.

Perhaps more important, there isn't much we can do with the genetic information. While progress is being made in areas such as pharmacogenetics—tailoring drug therapies based on an individual's genes—the advances haven't come at revolutionary speed. For example, a study published a few months ago [in 2012] described as the "largest body of pharmacogenetic data available to date," found that, in the context of depression drugs, "none of the more than 500,000 genetic mark-

The Cure for Genomic Therapy Hype

The infomercial-level hype for both gene therapy and stem cells is not just because scientists are trying to convince funders, but because they want to believe. Dr. Theodore Friedmann, professor of pediatrics at the University of California-San Diego Medical Center and the former president of the American Society of Gene and Cell Therapy, was a gene therapy pioneer. He says the nature of science is that what seem like sudden breakthroughs are usually preceded by years of persistent failure and incremental victory.

For example, successful organ transplantation took decades to achieve. Before doctors came up with a drug regime to get around the deadly problem of organ rejection. . . .

But he acknowledges his profession forgot these lessons when gene therapy first appeared: "Well-meaning scientists got carried away by their own enthusiasm and expressed this to patients desperately looking for help."

The cure for this—for both scientists and the public—is simple but not very appealing: humility and patience.

Emily Yoffe, Slate, *August 24, 2010.*

ers predicted treatment outcome." These results are, as suggested by the study authors, pretty sobering.

Changing Lifestyle

What about lifestyle change? The promotion of healthier lifestyles and preventive strategies are some of the most often articulated benefits of personal genomics. But there's little evidence that people can and will change their behaviour based on genetic risk information. A 2011 systematic review of all the available data found that the communication of genetic risk information "may have little or no effect on behaviour." And a 2012 study found that "genomic profiling for cancer risk prediction" is unlikely to have any significant impact on health.

You don't need to get your genome decoded to know you should exercise regularly, eat lots of fruits and vegetables and maintain a healthy weight. These are the kind of basic strategies (and the good sense to be born to wealthy and well-educated parents) that have the biggest impact. These actions don't need to be "personalized" through a high-tech and largely uninterpretable test.

For more than two decades, we've been told that we're in the midst of a genetic revolution. I'm still waiting. Meantime, if we really want to revolutionize our health, we should all put down the gene sequencers, fries and pop, pick up an apple and go for a brisk walk.

"*Only by harnessing our intellectual and financial resources nationally will we be able to realize the potential of stem cells as the therapeutic tool we all hope they will be.*"

Human Embryonic Stem Cell Research Can Meet Ethical Guidelines

Janet Rowley

Although scientists have developed adult stem cells they hope will cure serious genetic diseases, only embryonic stem cells will shed light on what exactly goes wrong with cell development, claims Janet Rowley in the following viewpoint. Using embryonic stem cells need not compromise the dignity of human life, she asserts. As long as donor consent is informed and research ends before cells develop complex structure, embryonic stem cell research is ethical, Rowley reasons. In truth, genetic scientists support ethical guidelines and oversight and concede that these elements should be included in embryonic stem cell policy conversations. Rowley, professor of medicine at the University of Chicago, is a member of the President's Council on Bioethics.

As you read, consider the following questions:

1. According to Rowley, what options are available to the parents of the 400,000 human embryos in the freezers of in vitro fertilization clinics?

2. In the author's opinion, by whom should all proposed embryonic stem cell research be reviewed to meet ethical guidelines?

3. What does the author claim is critical about state rules on the use of embryonic stem cells?

The decision to end many restrictions on embryonic stem cell research has removed a key barrier to research and discovery. Scientists are driven by the desire to succeed as fervently as our most success-driven businessmen, entrepreneurs, or lawyers. But for years they have contended with research limits that prevent innovation but do not serve a clear moral purpose. A responsible expansion of embryonic stem cell research can advance a vital goal—the search for new medical treatments—while respecting the dignity of human life.

A High Purpose

At present, there are about 400,000 human embryos in the freezers of in vitro fertilization clinics. Many are destined to be thawed and discarded and thus die. It is a true moral dilemma, but science offers a way to bring something good from a flawed situation. The parents of these embryos could allow them to die, or they could donate the embryos for research that someday might benefit patients with incurable diseases. This is a high purpose, one that promotes both human health and understanding.

Scientists have worked tirelessly to develop useful alternatives to these rare sources of embryonic stem cells. Through trial and error, they have developed a cocktail of genes that can transform adult human skin cells (from you and me) into cells closely resembling embryonic stem cells. But make no mistake—these are not embryonic stem cells. They are induced pluripotent stem cells.

The study of these cells is in its infancy. The hope is that induced pluripotent cells could be developed from individuals who have genetic disorders like juvenile diabetes, Parkinson's, and muscular dystrophy. Having stem cells with these defects could dramatically help scientists in their efforts to understand the basic, underlying problems in cells with these mutations. That's because stem cells offer a unique window into cell development—and they can shed light on how development goes awry in serious diseases. However, investigators also desperately need embryonic stem cells developed from patients with these genetic disorders to confirm that studies with induced pluripotent cells faithfully reproduce the genetic disorders. Scientists in the United States have developed such cell lines from embryos with genetic defects that were identified by genetic analyses. They have developed cell lines using money from private philanthropy because they have been prohibited by the previous administration from using federal money to carry out this important research.

A Need for Ethical Guidelines

Today, scientists are free of this impediment. But like all research, work on stem cells needs firm ethical guidelines. That's why scientists have joined with ethicists, lawyers, and patient advocates to develop the very strict rules that are currently in place to govern this area of study. I was part of a multidisciplinary group under the auspices of the National Academy of Sciences that met numerous times to develop guidelines that help ensure such work proceeds only within well-defined limits. The rules were adopted by California in 2005 to guide its stem cell initiative, and they have since been modified in response to California law and vigorous public debate.

© 2009 Steve Greenberg, Politicalcartoons.com/Cagle Cartoons Inc.

One of the guiding principles in these policies is the intrinsic value of human life. The guidelines call for careful ethical oversight of all research using human oocytes (eggs), embryos, or cell lines derived from these tissues. The cells and embryos must be obtained with informed consent, with no money paid for oocytes or embryos. All proposed research must be reviewed by a separate board that has scientists who are knowledgeable about embryonic stem cell research, as well as ethicists and the lay public. These representatives make certain that, for example, California's Institute for Regenerative Medicine, a state agency created by a 2004 stem cell research ballot referendum, supports only projects that advance knowledge and specifically require the use of human embryos—a high standard that ensures respect for human life. The embryos can be cultured for only 12 days under California's rules, meaning they never develop complex structure—a provision that many ethicists believe is important to prevent future experimentation on more mature embryos.

During this whole process of developing guidelines, scientists have been active and willing participants. Rather than demanding to do their work unfettered, scientists realize that strict guidelines will enable our society, which is supporting their work, to know that the research respects our shared values. Thus the scientific community now has many of the tools and resources needed to pursue stem cell research much more effectively than would have been possible only a few years ago.

A National Conversation

As we work to refine guidelines, it is critical that the rules be consistent between states, with national guidelines most likely issued by the National Institutes of Health. It is noteworthy that under President Bill Clinton, an eminent committee chaired by Shirley Tilghman (now president of Princeton University) wrote guidelines for NIH-funded stem cell research. The guidelines were due to take effect in 2001, but their implementation was canceled by President George W. Bush.

Everyone benefits when science works with the political system, rather than being kept at the margins. At a time when the promise and challenges of new technology are greater than ever, we need a national conversation driven by sound science and our common values. Scientists don't expect to dictate all the rules for stem cell research or for any field with complex moral issues. But we should have a clear voice in the democratic exchange, to help ensure that our research guidelines give us the best chance of finding new treatments and enriching life.

We've lost eight years; let's get started! Only by harnessing our intellectual and financial resources nationally will we be able to realize the potential of stem cells as the therapeutic tool we all hope they will be.

> "Not one person has been cured with embryonic stem cells."

Human Embryonic Stem Cell Cloning Has Failed to Yield Effective Cures

Michael Cook

In the following viewpoint Michael Cook claims that despite the early enthusiasm about the potential of embryonic stem cell cloning to cure debilitating diseases, no one has benefited from such a cure. In fact, the only thing memorable about embryonic stem cell research is the fraud perpetrated by a South Korean scientist who falsely claimed to have isolated embryonic stem cells. Sadly less celebrated, however, is the scientist who created stem cells from less controversial adult cells. Nevertheless, Cook concludes, some continue to pursue—without apology—an avenue that has yielded no cures. Cook is editor of MercatorNet, an Australian online publication that explores the ethical and moral implications of policy questions.

As you read, consider the following questions:

1. In Cook's opinion, how did scientists become political activists in the embryonic stem cell debate?

2. Why did bioethicists and scientists claim ethics had to take a back seat to science, in Cook's view?

3. According to the author, what form did some of the attacks on foes of embryo research take?

Let's wind the clock back to 2003. In January wheelchair-bound quadriplegic actor Christopher Reeve visited Australia to promote the legalisation of "therapeutic cloning". This was absolutely necessary, he said, or patients would die needlessly. Scepticism about the potential of embryonic stem cells was utterly unwarranted. "That's a myth," he told his Australian audience. "That's not true. Don't let anyone tell you it is a pipedream."

In July that year the *New England Journal of Medicine*, the world's leading medical journal, published a review article about the "promise of universal healing" in embryonic stem cells. "The Promethean prospect of eternal regeneration awaits us, while time's vulture looks on," the hyperventilating author wrote.

An Intense Debate

In short, people were excited. So excited, in fact, that in 2005 Australia passed legislation enabling "therapeutic cloning" for research purposes.

It's hard to recapture the intensity of that debate, in Australia and elsewhere. The cause was urgent. "We have lost so much time already, and I just really can't bear to lose any more," said former First Lady Nancy Reagan. Scientists became political activists. They lobbied politicians and insisted that therapeutic cloning would lead to cures for Parkinson's, Alzheimer's and diabetes. "I have never seen in my career a biological tool as powerful as the stem cells. It addresses every single human disease," said Hans Keirstead, of the University of California, Irvine.

Dissenters contended that adult stem cells already offered ethical avenues to cures and that embryonic stem cells would never work. Embryos were human beings and that it was moral madness to treat human life as a research tool. Women would be victims, too, as therapeutic cloning would require huge stocks of eggs. And besides, for a number of reasons, it just would not work.

The stakes were immense and the dissenters lost. Ethics had to take a back seat to science. Bioethicist Ruth Faden and stem cell scientist John Gearhart, both leaders in their field, spoke for many: "We believe that the obligation to relieve human suffering binds us all and justifies the instrumental use of early embryonic life."

But the cures never came.

Fraudulent and Unmemorable Research

In the past ten years the single most memorable event in embryonic stem cell research has been setting a world record for scientific fraud. In 2004 and 2005 *Science* published two papers by Hwang Woo-suk, a South Korean scientist. He claimed that he had successfully isolated human embryonic stem cells. Korea printed stamps in his honour and he was feted as an international celebrity. But he was a charlatan, his results were bogus and he had obtained human eggs unethically.

Press releases continued to gush from stem cell institutes, but they were always about promising developments rather than proven cures. In 2011, after many false starts and a year after launching a human trial for spinal cord injuries to cure people like Christopher Reeve, the California-based biotechnology firm Geron pulled the plug on all of its embryonic stem cell research to focus on cancer drugs. It had to: it was going broke.

The reason why stem cell research with embryos has faded from the headlines is that it has been superseded by "induced pluripotent stem cells". In 2007 Japanese researcher Shinya Yamanaka showed that it was possible to create stem cell lines from skin cells without destroying embryos. Almost immediately leading stem cell scientists abandoned embryonic stem cell research. Yamanaka—a man who had spurned embryonic stem cell research as unethical—won the Nobel Prize in Medicine last year [2012].

For various reasons some scientists continue to champion the cause of hESCs [human embryonic stem cells]. Earlier this month [May 2013] researchers at Oregon Health and Science University announced that they had cloned human embryos and successfully extracted embryonic stem cells. The study was published in the journal *Cell* after a lightning peer review. It was a "tour de force" and "an unparalleled achievement", said George Daly of the Harvard Stem Cell Institute.

His jubilation was short-lived.

The main effect of this paper was to evoke the nightmare of the Hwang [Woo-suk] scandal. Sharp-eyed readers noticed that some images had been duplicated. Clouds began to gather over the results. "It's a degree of sloppiness that you wouldn't expect in a paper that was going to have this high profile," an expert told *Nature*. "One worries if there is more than meets the eye and whether there are other issues with the work that are not as apparent."

The End of a Bioethical Battle

So this is the sputtering end of the greatest bioethical battle of the 21st century: just another blip of embarrassment in the 24/7 news cycle. As the *Boston Globe* has pointed out, "The emergence of reprogrammed stem cells, the difficulty of the involved method, and the obstacles to obtaining donor eggs for the procedure all make the advance more an important technical feat than a game-changer for stem cell scientists or a platform for new therapies."

Isn't it about time to establish a Stem Cell Truth and Reconciliation Commission? To get government funding so that they could play God with human embryos, scientists and bio-ethicists barnstormed, fibbed, exaggerated, hyped, and carica-tured. It was a brutal battle in which truth came second. "People need a fairy tale," said Ronald D.G. McKay, another leading stem cell scientist.

Foes of embryo research were called troglodytes and reli-gious fundamentalists. Their scientific credentials were ques-tioned. They were accused of being callous and indifferent to the suffering of patients with chronic illness.

And yet they were right.

Not one person has been cured with embryonic stem cells. Not one. There is still a long way to go before Yamanaka's cells can be used to treat patients. But the solution, when [it] comes, will not require the destruction of embryos.

Isn't anyone prepared to say, "Sorry"?

> *"If we think the gap between the haves and have-nots is large now, just wait until [genetic selection] technology is used to pre-select characteristics for success."*

Selecting a Child's Genetic Traits Will Create a Privileged Elite

Heather Long

Although some couples may use genetic selection techniques to ensure the viability of embryos used in the difficult process of in vitro fertilization, others may use the technique to select traits that would give their children advantages over others, argues Heather Long in the following viewpoint. To think that people would only use genetic selection to increase the chances of a successful in vitro pregnancy is naïve, she maintains. Wealthy families might choose to select traits such as height, health, looks, and intelligence, Long asserts. Because genetic screening is expensive, the high cost will leave those already struggling to compete further behind, she concludes. Long writes for the US edition of The Guardian, *a British newspaper.*

As you read, consider the following questions:

1. Why does Dagan Wells believe that people will not want to go through in vitro fertilization for something trivial?

2. What rhetorical question does Long ask about genetic design and Olympic competition?

3. What was the experience of those parents Long says could not afford in vitro fertilization?

When the world looks back at how the "designer babies" trend began, they will see an innocent start. A Philadelphia couple who had gone through the physical and emotional marathon of trying to have a child turned to intrauterine insemination and ultimately IVF [in vitro fertilization]. Like any rational people, they wanted to do everything to increase their chances that IVF would work. In this case, they sent the embryos to an Oxford lab, which ran a kind of minimal DNA test to see which embryos would be most likely to take.

It's hard to deny this Philadelphia couple the chance to be parents. David Levy and Marybeth Scheidts look very wholesome in their family photo holding their son Connor, born in May 2013. They clearly weren't trying to select the embryo with their preferred hair or eye color or other physical or mental traits. In fact, they didn't even have a full DNA analysis done, only a scan of the chromosomes, the structures that hold genes.

This isn't Brave New World–esque test tube babies. It's a traditional family—with the best of modern medicine.

But that's just it, not every couple will be like that.

Dagan Wells, the fertility specialist at Oxford University, told the Guardian:

> IVF is still expensive and uncomfortable with no guarantee of a baby at the end. I can't imagine many people wanting to go through the strains of IVF for something trivial.

A Frightening Progression

Wells has an entirely too charitable view of humanity. Perhaps he missed the news about the mother who loved tanning so much that she did it until she turned into a weird chestnut color and tried to bring her daughter along as well. Or the people who not only get plastic surgery for themselves, but also for their pets.

People do bizarre things to obtain a certain look, even if the most of us would say it's gross.

I can't imagine it will be long before some parents do ask the lab to give them a longer rundown of the genetic possibilities of each embryo. It will likely be a progression from just wanting a child, to wanting one less likely to get certain diseases, to wanting one more likely to have traits associated with being taller or more artistic or athletic. From there, it's not too hard to imagine something akin to the Subway sandwich line where you select different traits a la carte. And that's before anyone talks about the endless possibilities of combing DNA from more than two people.

There's a case to be made that genetic selection is just the next step in evolution. Who hasn't wanted to be a little bit taller or faster or smarter at some point? Who wouldn't want to give their child every advantage possible in an increasingly competitive world? And frankly, in the US, we've already done this kind of "designer baby" breeding for many crops and animals raised to be consumed. We have bred them and genetically modified them to be what we want (or, better said, what we think we want). Is it really that different to do the same for humans?

Genetic Haves and Have-Nots

For me, the answer is still yes, it is different for humans. Beyond the moral questions of "playing God", there are the practical ones. If this procedure takes off, it will only further exacerbate our world of haves and have-nots. IVF is expensive.

Cartoon by Grizelda. www.cartoonstock.com.

Many insurance providers in the US don't cover it. Even if the cost of this extra genetic screening comes down, the overall procedure is probably going to be out of reach for many Americans, let alone other countries around the world.

Imagine a scenario at a future Olympics: is it legitimate to have a genetically designed person competing against those who are not? At the moment, it's a bit of luck who has the right body for certain sports. But in the future, those traits could be selected for and groomed from the womb.

And that's to say nothing of other traits people in wealthy families might select for, creating a kind of demi-god race that will be taller, healthier, probably better-looking by conventional standards and more likely to have certain mental smarts. If the rest of the world is struggling to catch up now, imagine how much further behind they will be. A good college education will be an afterthought.

I have known a number of people who have undergone IVF, often multiple times, and I wouldn't want to deny them a better chance at having it work out the first time around. But I have also known couples who couldn't afford IVF. They ended up going the adoption route. They didn't get to select their child, especially those who adopted via the government-run foster care system. They felt fortunate even to be able to adopt one, regardless of the emotional or physical issues the child had or the outward characteristics.

Of course, it's worth celebrating the birth of a child to two Philadelphia parents who might not otherwise have had a kid. But if we think the gap between the haves and have-nots is large now, just wait until this technology is used to pre-select characteristics for success.

> "*Preimplantation genetic testing is 'unlikely to be useful as a method of positive selection. But it will have an expanding role in avoiding disease likelihood in children.'*"

Is China Really Breeding a Crop of Genetically Engineered Geniuses?

Will Oremus

Reports that China is engineering children with higher intelligence are more hype than reality, maintains Will Oremus in the following viewpoint. Although genetic selection will, in fact, give parents more options to choose healthier babies, success in genetically selecting babies with higher intelligence or physical attractiveness are unlikely, he asserts. Genetic scientists agree that the genetic contribution to intelligence is complex and so intertwined with environmental factors that the odds of designing an intelligent baby are mathematically low, he claims. Nevertheless, due to the ethical ramifications of genetic selection, Oremus concludes that the fact that this technology is distant is probably a good thing. Oremus is a staff writer for Slate.

As you read, consider the following questions:

1. What surprised Oremus about the response to the report that China was breeding genius babies?

2. Why does geneticist Santiago Munné believe that selecting embryos based on eye color is unethical?

3. According to the author, on what did evolutionary psychologist Geoffrey Miller base his assumption that the Chinese would implement a genetic-selection program?

Sexual reproduction is a genetic crapshoot. Out of hundreds of eggs and millions of sperm, one joins one to produce a baby whose natural endowments could reflect the best traits of both parents—or the absolute worst. To procreate through intercourse is to take a wild roll of the DNA dice. And the stakes could hardly be higher. One stray allele could mean the difference between a healthy baby and one with a debilitating disorder.

A Sensational Story

What if science offered a way to stack the odds in favor of a healthy, gifted child? The idea is as thrilling as it is alarming. But how realistic is it? Last week [March 2013], a widely shared story in the magazine *Vice* suggested it's imminent and inevitable—just not in the hidebound United States.

The article, headlined "China Is Engineering Genius Babies," reports that our superpower frenemies in the East have hatched a grand plan to breed a crop of hyperproductive smartypants. Here's an excerpt:

> At BGI Shenzhen, scientists have collected DNA samples from 2,000 of the world's smartest people and are sequencing their entire genomes in an attempt to identify the alleles which determine human intelligence. Apparently they're not far from finding them, and when they do, embryo screening will allow parents to pick their brightest zygote and poten-

tially bump up every generation's intelligence by five to 15 IQ points. Within a couple of generations, competing with the Chinese on an intellectual level will be like challenging Lena Dunham[1] to a getting-naked-on-TV contest.

You might think that such a sensational report would be received skeptically by readers and dismissed or debunked by the mainstream press. Instead it went viral on Facebook and Reddit and earned top billing in BBC Future's weekly "Best of the Web" roundup.

Sorting Through the Hype

In fact, key parts of the story are true—and not just the parts about Lena Dunham doffing her clothes. But large swaths are naïve, misleading, or grossly overstated. And it's worth sorting through them, because in the not-distant future, it's conceivable that parents will face a critical choice when it comes to making babies. The choice will be between fertilizing embryos in a lab and analyzing their DNA to try to select and gestate the healthiest possible baby, or doing it the old-fashioned way and leaving the genetics to chance.

Let's start with what's not true. China is not "engineering" babies. Even if it were, Chinese scientists wouldn't know how to genetically engineer a genius. And even if they did know how to genetically engineer a genius, the fact is that you can't ensure genius, because genius depends on environment as well as genes.

What is true, though, is fascinating, exciting, and troubling. Scientists are already developing the capacity to screen human embryos for a wide variety of genetic disorders, such as cystic fibrosis and sickle-cell anemia. At Reprogenetics, a private laboratory in New Jersey, couples who carry a genetic disease can have their embryos checked for the mutation before implanting them in the woman's uterus. The process is

---

1. Actress Lena Dunham is known for often appearing naked in the television show *Girls*.

referred to as preimplantation genetic diagnosis, and the technology is advancing rapidly. Santiago Munné, the lab's director, told me that within a year he expects to be able to offer embryo analyses that screen for more than 100 diseases at once, for a few thousand dollars.

Women are already using preimplantation analysis to select the gender of their embryos. And in the United States, they're overwhelmingly choosing to have daughters.

Opening the Door to Broader Screening

The next leap will be to whole-genome sequencing of embryos. That opens the door to screening not just for sex or single-gene disorders but for more complex disorders like autism—or even, conceivably, qualities like physical attractiveness or intelligence. Munné considers this type of "positive selection" beyond the pale: "Selecting for embryos based on eye color, etc., means you are discarding the others based on traits, and that's unethical."

But not everyone shares his qualms. The premise of the *Vice* story is that the Chinese government is eager to identify the alleles, or genetic variations, that most closely correlate with high IQ scores, so that the country's parents can select from a number of their own embryos on the basis of intelligence. That isn't loading the genetic dice, exactly, because the parents can't change their own genes. And it isn't engineering, per se, because it doesn't involve manipulating the genes of the offspring. (That may also be possible someday, but most experts believe it's further off.) It's more like rolling the dice 10 times and then getting to choose from among the resulting combinations.

That's still a powerful prospect. As NYU evolutionary psychologist Geoffrey Miller—a participant in the Chinese genome-sequencing study—tells *Vice*, "Even if it only boosts the average kid by five IQ points, that's a huge difference in terms of economic productivity, the competitiveness of the country, how many patents they get, how their businesses are run, and how innovative their economy is."

Where *Vice* goes astray is in the article's blithe insinuation that this is all right around the corner. It's true that BGI Shenzhen has embarked on a research project to find relationships between genes and IQ. But experts say the implication that a handful of specific genetic variations "determine human intelligence" is spurious, let alone the claim that "apparently they're not far from finding them." Intelligence, you see, isn't just a matter of a few alleles here and there.

A Matter of Math

Hank Greely, director of Stanford's Center for Law and the Biosciences, says preimplantation genetic screening could one day render procreation via sex obsolete, at least for those who can afford it. But that doesn't mean it will result in a generation of geniuses. "I think it's pretty clear that intelligence—if it even exists as an entity, which remains controversial among psychologists—involves a boatload of genes and genetic combinations, all of them substantially mediated through the environment. The chances that genetic selection is going to lead to really substantial increases in human intelligence in your lifetime are low."

Munné agrees. "IQ is controlled by probably more than 1,000 genes, so there is no point even trying to control for that," he says.

The problem is simple math, adds Lee Silver, a genetics expert and molecular biologist at Princeton. Even if you could pinpoint a handful of genes that were likely to result in a higher IQ, the chances of any given embryo containing the right combination are minuscule. "Add in the fact that nongenetic factors account for 40 to 50 percent of the variance of something like intelligence," and the project is basically hopeless. The bottom line, he says: Preimplantation genetic testing is "unlikely to be useful as a method of positive selection. But it will have an expanding role in avoiding disease likelihood in children."

In any case, there's no evidence that BGI Shenzhen or the Chinese government is actually planning to try to use the study's findings to implement some kind of genetic-selection program. Miller, the sole source cited in the *Vice* story, tells me he was basing that assumption on "my speculation based on the history of Chinese population policy" combined with "off-the-record discussions with a couple of people involved." At this point, it's just an academic study.

While Miller agrees that aspects of the *Vice* story may have been framed a little sensationally, he defends the idea that embryo selection could eventually lead to significant gains in intelligence. "The key point is that the [BGI Shenzhen] project is not just looking for a handful of genes to genetically manipulate," he says. "They're looking for the millions of genetic variations that contribute to intelligence and how they add up in aggregate. That's what gives you the potential power to do the embryo selection."

Even those who disagree with Miller about intelligence think it makes sense to start grappling with the ethical implications of preimplantation genetic screening today. Silver, for one, counts himself as an advocate of the procedure, at least in certain cases. "In my opinion, even a partially informed choice is always better than chance," he says. "Those who reject this point of view often don't think of the natural process as chance, but rather as God or Mother Nature doing her work. But as I said to Stephen Colbert on his show, 'Mother Nature is a nasty bitch.'"

Yet the line between screening for disorders and selecting for traits can be blurry. If it's OK to screen for Down syndrome, is it OK to screen for a genetic predisposition to alcoholism, depression, or obesity? Where do you draw the line between developmental disabilities and low IQ? Maybe it's a good thing that the ability to build genius babies is a long way off. That should give us some time to decide what's worse—a risky dice roll or a rigged game.

> *"There is a real possibility . . . that [genetic manipulation] will work for athletes in the future because we have some of the best brains in medicine working on it."*

Antidoping Agencies Anticipate Genetic Enhancement to Improve Athletic Performance

John Naish

Superhuman athletic performances gain the attention of antidoping agencies whose goal is to ensure fair competition. Some fear that these seemingly superhuman athletes may use genetic enhancement to improve their performance, asserts John Naish in the following viewpoint. Indeed, studies show that genetic modification make mice run longer and gain less weight. Researchers believe that viruses with cells genetically designed to improve blood cell production or muscle-building hormones could improve athletic performance, Naish suggests. Unfortunately, he claims, gene doping will be difficult to detect as modified cells operate in the same way as natural cells. Naish is a staff writer for the Daily Mail, *a British newspaper.*

As you read, consider the following questions:

1. According to Naish, what 2012 Olympic performance prompted claims of genetic enhancement?

2. What discovery made gene therapy possible?

3. In the author's opinion, what is the penalty to pay for maintaining a bank of athlete blood samples available for retesting?

The controversy over Chinese swimmer Ye Shiwen's astonishing gold medal performance this week [August 2012] is no longer confined to just the suspicions of drug abuse, which she emphatically denies.

It has raised concerns about another worrying—and infinitely more sinister—threat to the world of honest competition: the genetic enhancement of athletes.

Questioning Superior Athletic Performance

John Leonard, the highly respected American director of the World Swimming Coaches Association, described the 16-year-old's world-record-breaking performance as 'suspicious', 'disturbing' and 'unbelievable'.

'Any time someone has looked like superwoman in the history of our sport they have later been found guilty of doping,' he added.

He went on to say that the authorities who tested Ye Shiwen for drug abuse should also check to see 'if there is something unusual going on in terms of genetic manipulation'.

A Chinese anti-doping official, Jiang Zhixue, described Leonard's claims as completely unreasonable.

The astonishing suggestion seems to be that London 2012 may be the first Olympics in which competitors are attempting to cheat by altering their genes to build muscle and sinew, and boost their blood's oxygen-carrying powers.

The Threat of Frankenstein Athletes

The chilling comment from one of the world's top coaches seems to herald the possibility of Frankenstein athletes, of an unbeatable master-race of genetically manipulated super-competitors with enhanced lung-power, or heightened strength, or some other characteristic that enables them to snatch medal after medal from honest competitors.

And while this might appear to belong to the world of science-fiction, scientists are taking the threat seriously.

Dr Ted Friedmann, chair of the genetics panel of the World Anti-Doping Agency [WADA], said he "would not be surprised at all" if gene enhancement were not now being secretly used by some competitors.

He has been working to find ways to detect "gene doping" and prevent it from becoming common. "The technology is ripe for abuse," he warned.

But can athletes—or trainers—really enhance their performance through genetic means?

Laboratory experiments have already shown that the science can work. In 2005, Ronald Evans, a hormone expert working at the Salk Institute of Biological Studies in La Jolla, California, showed how genetic modification can increase the athletic power of mice.

Evans produced a group of genetically modified mice with an increased amount of slow-twitch muscle fibre. This type of fibre is associated with strong cardiovascular muscles and boosts an athlete's endurance.

Evans's mice could run for an hour longer than normal mice, were resistant to weight gain no matter what they were fed on, and remained at peak fitness even when they took no exercise. A form of genetic modification is already being tested in medicine, in the form of gene therapy for diseases such as cystic fibrosis.

Rapidly Advancing Knowledge

Genetically engineered athletes are still a distant reality. Yet the knowledge of how genotype is related to certain aspects of health is advancing rapidly. The time may not be far off when genotype could be used as an additional tool to identify performance potential, or shape training, nutrition and drugging regimens. The counterpoint is that this advancing knowledge will also provide new weapons in the fight against doping, whether genetic or not.

Cristina Velloso, Biologist, *June 2012.*

Gene Modification Techniques

Most gene modification techniques involve placing genetically modified DNA inside a virus and injecting it into the human body. The virus then enters human cells, and its modified DNA attaches itself to the human DNA inside those cells.

Gene therapy is at a very early stage in development and has become possible as a result of our discovery in 2003 of how to map the human genome.

This meant we could identify specific genes that cause disease—cystic fibrosis is caused by one faulty gene, for example, and the idea is that gene therapy can replace the faulty gene with one that works.

In the same way, it may well be possible for athletes to use a virus to introduce a gene that spurs the production of oxygen-carrying red blood cells or muscle-building hormones. And the heightened blood-cell counts or hormone levels might simply appear to the doping agencies to be the product of an extraordinary athlete's body.

Testing for Gene Doping

Tests are being developed to detect this kind of manipulation, but at the moment, the World Anti-Doping Agency does not have one.

Anna Baoutina, a senior research scientist at the National Measurement Institute in Sydney, told the Tackling Doping In Sport conference in London earlier this year [2012] that no gene test was in place for the [Summer] Olympics.

"The major advantage of gene doping is that it is very difficult to detect compared to drug doping. The doping gene is very similar to natural cells found in the body," she told journalists. "We are developing methods to fight it."

Olympics leaders say, however, that they are confident they will soon be able to detect the first generations of genetically super-powered cheats.

For example, Patrick Schamasch, medical director of the International Olympic Committee (IOC), has said that the viruses used to smuggle genes into the body leave behind traces which can be detected. But this will probably not be the case for long, he warned: "I'm certain viruses will be invented that won't leave traces."

Instead, Olympics officials are banking on the success of their newly introduced "biological passport." This keeps track of the athlete's overall physiological profile, and triggers [an] alarm if anything about it changes in a suspicious manner—for example if their everyday hormone levels take an unusual leap.

Many scientists, though, question the authorities' confidence in their ability to catch dopers and point out that cheats are already using biological methods to avoid detection.

In particular they are concerned about the lack of a test for an increasingly popular form of cheating—a blood transfusion where athletes store pints of their own blood and re-inject them later, before a race, for example.

This boosts the number of oxygen-carrying red cells in the blood, improving power and stamina. But it is hard to detect such transfusions, because they involve the athlete's own blood, so don't contain traces of any foreign body. The WADA has funded research into developing a test for the transfusions, but it is still not ready.

Professor Dominic Wells, a gene therapy researcher who has studied the possibility of modifying athletes, believes we are still some way off being able to use genes to significantly change athletes' performance.

"There is a real possibility, however, that this will work for athletes in the future because we have some of the best brains in medicine working on it," he says.

If genetic manipulation does become common, the Olympic doping authorities at least have time on their side.

Retrospective Testing

New cheating methods will always remain undetected until the authorities develop scientific methods of spotting them. Olympic chiefs have therefore decided to keep medal-winners' blood samples for eight years, so they can subject them to new tests when they are developed.

Last week [August 2012], for example, Arne Ljungqvist, the anti-doping chief of the International Olympic Committee, disclosed that about 100 samples from the Athens Games in 2004 had been retested—and six athletes who competed have been identified as possible drug cheats. "The longer you wait the better, if you want to catch someone," he said.

There is, however, a real penalty to pay for this. Whenever we cheer a new champion on the podium, we must always wonder whether their shiny medal will be taken back in ignominy years down the line.

The idea of retrospective testing tarnishes Olympic achievement. But if that is the price we have to pay to keep the spectre of genetically-modified, unbeatable Franken[stein]-athletes at bay, then sadly, it does seem to be worth paying.

"There is no documented case of genetic
techniques having been used to enhance
athletic ability in people."

How Close Are We to Gene Doping?

Theodore Friedmann

Gene doping—the genetic enhancement of athletic perfor-
mance—presumes that gene therapy methods that hope to cure
genetic diseases could improve athletic performance, claims The-
odore Friedmann in the following viewpoint. However, suspi-
cions that some athletes benefit from genetic enhancement re-
main unproven. Genetic manipulation is a complex, risky, and
highly experimental process, Friedmann maintains. Nevertheless,
he concludes, some athletes, trainers, and sports doctors rarely
wait for tests proving a performance-enhancing technique's safety
or effectiveness before using it. Friedmann is director of the Cen-
ter for Molecular Genetics at the University of California at San
Diego School of Medicine.

As you read, consider the following questions:

1. On what principle is the movement to evade the international effort to curb doping in sport founded, in
Friedmann's opinion?

Theodore Friedmann, "How Close Are We to Gene Doping?," *Hasting Center Report*,
March/April 2010, pp. 20–21. Copyright © 2010 by The Hastings Center. All rights reserved. Reproduced by permission.

2. What instances does the author cite that can be interpreted as serious attempts gene doping?

3. What are some of the questions the author raises about the idea of genetically bringing all athletes to the same level of capability?

We know from the third law of motion described in the midseventeenth century by Sir Isaac Newton in his *Principia Mathematica* that every action in the physical universe generates an equal and opposite reaction. That's what enables fish to swim, birds to fly, rockets to soar. It's what allows us to sit quietly in chairs without falling through the floor or floating off into space. It seems to me very likely that the Newtonian laws of motion also explain some aspects of the emergence and evolution of new concepts. A prime example might be a nettlesome new cottage industry that has arisen to evade the international effort to curb doping in sports.

This new movement is founded on the position that it is the very existence of antidoping regulation and oversight that produces a climate of cheating and distrust in sports, and that regulation and prohibition should be replaced by a more laissez-faire approach.[1] This argument would lead us to accept *all* methods for enhancing performance outside of those permitted by the rules of that sport—drugs, supplements, materials, surgery, and now gene-based enhancement—should be allowed, even encouraged and valued. Some have even suggested that our society has a moral duty to promote active and unregulated use of any and all methods to achieve athletic "excellence." Bizarrely, one prominent proponent of this approach labels such a process "natural."[2]

As troublesome as traditional, drug-based doping has long been, the emergence of gene doping is seen by some to represent an ominous new opportunity in cheating technology.[3] The concept of gene doping grew out of the important development in the early 1970s of a novel approach in medicine that promised to treat human disease by attacking underlying genetic defects. Thus was born the idea of gene therapy.[4] In early, phase I safety studies, gene therapy has produced effective treatments for a number of diseases, such as pediatric immune deficiency, a genetic form of blindness, and neurodegeneration,[5] with more sure to come in the very near future. While the efficacy of treatments has not yet been confirmed in more extensive phase III studies, the success so far teaches us is that it is clearly possible to introduce new genetic functions into human beings in forms efficient and stable enough to modify traits that produce serious disease and thus to ameliorate life-threatening illness and ease suffering.

The same methods can undoubtedly be used to enhance normal human traits, including traits that affect athletic ability. One might readily envision genetic modification of healthy young athletes to augment functions useful for athletic performance, such as muscle growth and contraction, endurance, blood production, pain perception, and oxygen delivery to exercising muscle. But how close we are to gene doping in sports is a matter of debate.

When the concept of gene doping first emerged a decade or so ago, some critics considered it improbable and far from imminent. One of my most respected colleagues, who had a prominent role in the gene therapy oversight process, called the potential for using genetic modification methods for gene doping "a lot of gale-force hand waving." In contrast, others saw it to be the obvious next and inevitable step in doping and cheating technology and believed it offered potential advantages over drug-based doping—that it might be more effective and more difficult to detect. Many feared that gene doping would enter the world of competitive sports very quickly; in fact, the sports media have predicted that every Olympic Games in the last decade would probably be the first genetically doped games.

Indeed, several instances have come to light that can only be interpreted as serious attempts at gene doping. An athletic coach in Germany was found to be making diligent efforts to obtain a gene vector called Repoxygen that contains and expresses the erythropoietin gene and was developed to increase blood production in patients with serious diseases such as cancer and chronic kidney disease. The product of the gene, erythropoietin, is in fact one of the most widely used drugs in the world for treatment of these disorders and, of course, is known to be heavily abused in some endurance sports, such as cycling. One imagines that the intended use of this material by the coach might have been other than for research on gene-based treatment of diseases. In addition, shortly before the Beijing Games in 2008, a German investigative television team broadcast a program identifying a Chinese scientist who was reported to be offering genetic manipulation for athletes.

Even though many suspect genetic doping among athletes who have performed feats that seem to lie outside of normal human physiological boundaries in Olympic and other elite sporting events, these suspicions have never been confirmed. There is no documented case of genetic techniques having been used to enhance athletic ability in people. We do know that genetic manipulations have produced mice and, in some cases, primates with enhanced traits crucial for athletic performance, including increased muscle function, prolonged endurance, and elevated blood production. If gene therapy is becoming increasingly feasible and available and if the pressure for gene doping is so great, why has it not yet been documented in athletes?

One reason may be that the procedures for safe, successful, and legitimate genetic manipulation for medical purposes are extremely complicated, lying outside the capability of most rogue operations. Even though the production of gene doping materials is achievable using standard graduate school or even undergraduate molecular biology technology, the truly difficult aspect of gene therapy is its execution: bringing about the safe and effective performance of complicated human clinical manipulations by methods consistent with international ethical standards of human clinical work. Even for legitimate gene therapy, it has taken several decades of experimental refinement and testing to learn how to express added genetic information safely in human patients. For those with medically urgent conditions—such as severe combined immunodeficiency or adrenoleukodystrophy, a rare fatal brain disease—the risks of using still imperfect and even dangerous tools to ameliorate disease and ease suffering are ethically justified. Gene therapy remains a highly experimental and potentially risky technique, and even some of the successful therapies have caused serious side effects, including leukemia and even death.

Another possible reason for the absence of documented human gene doping lies in the flawed logic of some of the justifications for its development. Genetic and other pharmacological manipulations are often rationalized as attempts to bring all athletes to the same base level of capability, evening out all innate gene-based traits and ignoring that glaring fact that we do not understand the multiple genetic, environmental, and acquired traits that shape athletic "talent"—ambition, educational and economic opportunities, and the "fire in the belly" component, for instance—well enough to even begin to "level" them. On its face, such an extreme leveling seems an impossible task. And yet, even if all athletes could be brought to a "level playing field" genetically, physically, environmentally, and socially, wouldn't all be expected to perform identically? Where then is the sport? Where is the competition? Who gets the gold medal and the lucrative endorsements—the "athlete" or the molecular biologist sitting on the sidelines?

We know from vast experience that, like all technology, the use of apparently sophisticated genetic doping methods will not await demonstration of safety, much less efficacy, before being applied in sports. For that reason, the World Anti-

Doping Agency [WADA] has included genetic doping in its list of banned methods since 2004 and has instituted major research projects to identify potential methods for gene doping and for detection. And yet, those intent on using illicit methods are likely to pay little attention to WADA lists or to comply with the multiple layers of local and national oversight and regulation required for gene therapy—review and approval of local institutional review boards, human subjects committees, and federal oversight and regulatory bodies like the National Institutes of Health's Recombinant DNA Advisory Committee and the Food and Drug Administration. The financial and other rewards are too great and the sources of funding too deep in sports for those intent on gene doping to be concerned about such troublesome niceties.

It seems inevitable that genetic tools for doping will eventually be developed and applied. There is little question that attempts at gene doping will be made at an increasing pace in the near future. But the perpetrators will almost certainly fail, probably technically and certainly ethically, and they will do medical mischief in the process. In the course of their premature misadventures, they are far more likely to do harm than to provide athletic advantage.

Sport is a deeply human activity dependent on an honest and transparent rule-based "contract" between participants. Those who love it deserve protection from those who would weaken or destroy its rules and introduce unethical, ineffective, and probably harmful materials and tools. Those who practice genetic manipulation, evading requirements for ethical and scientific review and applying genetic tools without full disclosure and informed consent, should certainly be considered guilty of scientific or medical malpractice and professional misconduct.

Notes

1. J. Tierney, "Let the Games be Doped," *New York Times*, August 14, 2008; N. Fost, "Let the Doping Begin," *New York Times*, August 12, 2008; "A Level Playing

Field?" *Nature* 454 (2008): 667.

2. A. Miah, "Enhanced Athletes: It's Only Natural," *Washington Post*, August 1, 2008.

3. T. Friedmann et al., "Gene Doping and Sport," *Science* 327 (2010): 647–48.

4. T. Friedmann and R. Roblin, "Gene Therapy for Human Genetic Disease?" *Science* 175 (1972): 949–55.

5. S. Hacein-Bey-Abina et al., "Sustained Correction of X-Linked Severe Combined Immunodeficiency by Ex Vivo Gene Therapy," *New England Journal of Medicine* 346 (2002): 1185–93; A. Aiuti et al., "Gene Therapy for Immunodeficiency Due to Adenosine Deaminase Deficiency," *New England Journal of Medicine* 360 (2009): 447–58; A.M. Maguire et al., "Safety and Efficacy of Gene Transfer for Leber's Congenital Amaurosis," *New England Journal of Medicine* 358 (2008): 2240–48; N. Cartier et al., "Hematopoietic Stem Cell Gene Therapy with a Lentiviral Vector in X-Linked Adrenoleukodystrophy," *Science* 326 (2009): 818–23.

Periodical and Internet Sources Bibliography

The following articles have been selected to supplement the diverse views presented in this chapter.

| Elizabeth Allen | "Study of Role Genes Play in Disease Advances," *San Antonio Express-News*, April 1, 2010. |

Daphne Chia — "The Alternative to a Cloned or Genetically Enhanced Child," *Asian Bioethics Review*, March 2013.

Marcia Clemmitt — "Genes and Health," *CQ Researcher*, January 21, 2011.

David King — "Human Stem Cell Cloning: 'Holy Grail' or Techno-fantasy?" CNN.com, May 17, 2013.

Gina Kolata — "Cancer Fight: Unclear Tests for New Drug," *New York Times*, April 19, 2010.

Sheldon Krimsky — "On Designer Babies," *Tufts Medicine*, Summer 2012.

Timothy Maher — "Reshaping the Human Species," *Technology Review*, July/August 2012.

Philip M. Rosoff — "I'll Be a Monkey's Uncle: A Moral Challenge to Human Genetic Enhancement Research," *Journal of Medical Ethics*, April 2011.

Christiana Velloso — "Designer Athletes," *Biologist*, June 2012.

Helen Wallace — "We Are Wrong to Use Genetic Manipulation for Future Health," *The Guardian*, 2011.

Emily Yoffe — "The Medical Revolution: Where Are the Cures Promised by Stem Cells, Gene Therapy, and the Human Genome?," *Slate*, August 24, 2010.

OPPOSING
VIEWPOINTS®
SERIES

Should Biotech Companies Be Allowed to Patent Human Genes?

Chapter Preface

One of several controversies surrounding human gene patents is whether patent holders should be required to license their use to others. Indeed, several analysts argue that the focus of the June 2013 US Supreme Court decision in *Association for Molecular Pathology v. Myriad Genetics* was misplaced. The court decided that companies could not patent human genes as genes are naturally occurring. However, some commentators claim that the actual problem was not that Myriad Genetics had patented human genes but that the company ruthlessly pursued its patents to the detriment of those who would benefit. Myriad Genetics obtained patents on two genes linked to breast cancer: BRCA1 and BRCA2. The company aggressively blocked other companies from using the genes, which allowed Myriad to control the lucrative breast cancer test market.

In truth, US patent law places few restrictions on patent holders, who have almost complete freedom to decide whether or not to license their patents to others. However, because the lawsuit against Myriad focused on whether a company had the right to patent a human gene, the Supreme Court decision left open the licensing concern. Women's health groups were more concerned that the patent limited research on the breast cancer genes and access to testing. Moreover, while the court ruled that isolated DNA could not be patented, it held that companies could patent complementary DNA (cDNA)—a synthetically created gene segment. Whether companies will license these discoveries remains a controversial question. Some argue that they should be freely shared, and others claim that laws requiring licensing are unnecessary.

Among those who believe that genetic discoveries should be made widely available is Francis Collins, a physician-geneticist noted for his discoveries of disease genes and his leadership of the Human Genome Project. Director of the National Institutes of Health (NIH), Collins asserts, "You don't want to put toll booths on basic science."[1] In fact, when he discovered the gene linked to cystic fibrosis in 1989, Collins insisted that the discovery be available to any laboratory interested in testing. Moreover, in his 2009 book *Language of Life: DNA and the Revolution in Personalized Medicine*, Collins contrasts his approach with Myriad's choice—challenging any lab that wanted to offer breast cancer testing.

Some claim the court did not address the licensing issue as only Congress can do so. The Patent and Trade Law Amendments of 1980—also known as the Bayh-Dole Act—did in fact allow federal agencies that fund research to require patent holders to license their discoveries to others if any one of four criteria are met. One criteria is failure to satisfy consumer health needs, which in the eyes of some would apply to Myriad's refusal to allow licenses for confirmation or second-opinion breast cancer testing. However, the NIH has thus far declined to exercise its power. Some European governments have been more proactive. A 2004 Swiss law allows a court to grant a compulsory license if the holder engages in anticompetitive practices. A 2005 Belgian law allows the government to grant a license for a patent-protected invention in the interest of public health. Efforts in the United States, however, have met with resistance. Florida US congressional representative Debbie Wasserman Schultz, a breast cancer survivor, sponsored a bill that would require genetic diagnostic labs to license their patents for confirmation or second-opinion testing. Although women's health groups supported the bill, the American Civil Liberties Union opposed the law as too weak. The America Invents Act did, however, require that the Patent and Trademark Office study the impact of patents on genetic diagnostics. The office has yet to submit its report.

1. Quoted in Ken Garber, "Homestead 2000: The Genome," *Signals*, March 3, 2000.

Despite these obstacles, Duke University genomic ethics professor Robert Cook-Deegan believes licensing should be compulsory. "It's a point of pushback against really egregious business practices,"[2] Cook-Deegan claims. However, Myriad representatives disagree. According to Benjamin G. Jackson, Myriad's senior director for legal affairs, "There's no evidence whatsoever that a solution as dramatic as compulsory licensing is anywhere near necessary, warranted, or desirable on any level."[3] Moreover, argues University of Michigan law professor Rebecca Eisenberg, the biotechnology industry is likely to oppose any broad legislation requiring companies to license patent-protected genetic testing. "That's a nonstarter with the biotechnology industry,"[4] she maintains.

Whether licensing of genetic-testing patents should be mandatory remains a controversial question in the human genetics debate. The authors in the following chapter debate other issues concerning gene patents in examining the question of whether biotech companies should be allowed to patent human genes. Whether Congress will enact mandatory licensing legislation remains to be seen.

2. Quoted in Kenneth Jost, "Patenting Human Genes," *CQ Researcher*, May 31, 2013.
3. *Ibid.*
4. *Ibid.*

> *"The private sector has developed ways to balance the strong incentives provided by patents with the desire for progress in the field of human genetics and medicine."*

Gene Patents Promote Scientific Progress and Medical Innovation

Lawrence Horn and Kristin Neuman

According to Lawrence Horn and Kristin Neuman in the following viewpoint, the United States is the world leader in biotechnology and health care due, in part, to patent protection. Unfortunately, they argue, flawed claims that isolated human genes are naturally occurring and are thus not patentable threaten scientific progress. Indeed, the research to isolate these genes requires significant investment that patents encourage. Moreover, medicines such as insulin and human growth hormone are synthetic proteins made with patented DNA constructs. Claims that patents restrict research and medical innovation are unfair, when, in truth, researchers have come together to make diagnostic patent rights available to all, Horn and Neuman conclude.

Horn is president and CEO of MPEG LA, which operates Librassay, a patent licensing facility at which former biotech patent lawyer Neuman is executive director.

As you read, consider the following questions:

1. According to Horn and Neuman, how long has the US patent office been granting patents on manmade DNA constructs?

2. In what section of the US Constitution did the Founding Fathers mandate the patent system?

3. Which are some of the institutions that support the Librassay initiative, according to the authors?

The greatest dangers to liberty lurk in the insidious encroachment by men of zeal, well meaning but without understanding. —*Louis D. Brandeis*

Just a few words and little thought separate yet another stronghold of the American economy from ruin. It doesn't have to be that way. The U.S. patent system has made America's biotech and pharmaceutical industries the envy of the world.

This month [April 2013], the U.S. Supreme Court heard oral arguments in a case posing the question: "Are human genes patentable?" The very way the ACLU [American Civil Liberties Union] and other petitioners have worded the question sets up an emotional red herring designed to solicit false choices. The patents at issue in the case do not cover genes in a human body. They cover man-made DNA constructs with specific properties and functions not found in nature. The artificial constructs are used to detect mutations in human genes and to diagnose a patient's risk for developing breast and ovarian cancer.

The Consequences of Losing Patent Protection

The biotech industry was spawned with the advent of recombinant DNA technology in the early 1980s. As a result, treatments, diagnostic assays, and gene therapies have been developed for countless diseases and disorders. Without patent protection, many believe that innovation in scientific fields that rely on the discovery and use of DNA would come to a screeching halt because there would be less incentive to invest in these areas.

Joan Ellis, Scientist, June 18, 2013.

The Cost of a Red Herring

The cost of diving into the pseudo-scientific swamp created by the petitioners could be substantial. The U.S. Patent Office has been granting patents on man-made DNA constructs for nearly 30 years. Today, the United States is the world leader in biotechnology and health care—in no small part due to a long history of robust incentives for innovation investment based on stable and reliable patent protection. Yet taking the bait proffered by the ACLU would put that at risk.

The emotional red herring does not stop there. The ACLU maintains that if we continue to reward scientific progress with these patents, then researchers and health care providers will be prevented from using the patented inventions to further scientific research and medical product innovation. This, too, presents a false choice. Patents and scientific progress can coexist in genetic medicine. In fact, they already do.

Artificial DNA constructs like those at issue in the case represent the very best reasons for patent protection. Insulin, human growth hormone and erythropoietin are just three of the many synthetic protein therapies made using artificial DNA constructs. Likewise, artificial DNA constructs serve as a basis for new diagnostic tests, particularly in the field of cancer, as well as new vaccines, and have other important applications in agriculture, food safety, industrial materials, energy and environmental biotechnology. But without some means to protect the enormous investment they require, breakthrough products and services like these may never come to be.

Our Founding Fathers had the foresight to provide this means through the patent system mandated by the U.S. Constitution (Article 1, Section 8, Clause 8) securing to "inventors the exclusive right to their discoveries" for a limited time in order "to promote the progress of science and useful arts." As Abraham Lincoln explained, patents add "the fuel of interest to the fire of genius, in the discovery and production of new and useful things."

Patents and Progress

Patent protection and scientific progress go hand in hand. The marketplace has proved adept at providing access to patented DNA constructs to further scientific progress because of patent protection, not in spite of it. Since the patents in the case were granted, according to the respondents in the case, "over 18,000 researchers have conducted studies on the BRCA 1/2 genes,[1] published over 8,000 papers, and conducted over 130 clinical trials." In short, this state of affairs illustrates the very dissemination of science and knowledge envisioned by the Constitution—a far cry from the secrecy surrounding scientific discovery and the diversion of private investment dollars to other technologies and other countries, to which the petitioners' position would lead.

1. BRCA1 is a gene found in all humans that produces a protein responsible for repairing DNA. Damaged BRCA1 cannot repair damaged DNA properly, increasing cancer risk. BRCA2, while structurally different from BRCA1, also produces a protein necessary to pair DNA. Damaged variations of these genes increase risks for breast cancer as part of a hereditary breast-ovarian cancer syndrome.

What's more, forward-looking patent holders and leaders in health care research—the Johns Hopkins University, Ludwig Institute for Cancer Research, Memorial Sloan-Kettering Cancer Center, the National Institutes of Health and others—have come together to support Librassay, a private market initiative making diagnostic patent rights available on the same terms to anyone, while giving patent owners the opportunity for wide adoption of their technologies, reasonable compensation for their investments, and the incentive to invest more. The Librassay initiative is growing and is expected to accelerate innovation in diagnostics and personalized medicine.

In the gene patent case before the Supreme Court, the rhetoric does not match the reality. Working with the patent system as it has existed for 30 years, the private sector has developed ways to balance the strong incentives provided by patents with the desire for progress in the field of human genetics and medicine. It is the reason why the biotech and medical industries have thrived in America. The Supreme Court would do well to find a way to maintain the status quo and avoid the emotional appeal of false choices.[2]

---

2. On June 13, 2013, in *Association for Molecular Pathology v. Myriad Genetics*, Supreme Court Justice Clarence Thomas, writing for the majority, held that "A naturally occurring DNA segment is a product of nature and not patent eligible merely because it has been isolated, but cDNA is patent eligible because it is not naturally occurring." cDNA is DNA that is synthesized in a complex process.

"The very idea that a biotech company could hold a monopoly on a piece of the human genome (let alone a test) was offensive to most of us lay folks."

Gene Patents Allow Biotech Companies to Monopolize Human Genes

Robin Abcarian

Human gene patents allowed biotech company Myriad Genetics to monopolize genetic tests that provide women with useful information about their chances of developing breast cancer, claims Robin Abcarian in the following viewpoint. Myriad's relentless pursuit of its patents led to a lawsuit that raised the human gene patent question, she reports. Myriad forced competitive geneticists to stop giving breast cancer gene tests to their patients, Abcarian asserts. Fortunately, the US Supreme Court concluded that biotech companies could not patent human genes, rejecting the patent owner's claim that the isolated gene does not occur naturally in the human body. Abcarian is a national correspondent for the Los Angeles Times.

As you read, consider the following questions:

1. How did actress and activist Angelina Jolie bring attention to the human gene patent question?

2. How much did Myriad spend before it turned a profit on its patented test?

3. How did Myriad defend charges that it forced geneticists to stop administering genetic tests?

In the course of our country's history, the U.S. Patent and Trademark Office has bestowed coveted protection on many strange and wondrous inventions: the three-legged pantyhose (in case one leg runs), the sealed, circular peanut-butter-and-jelly sandwich, the motorized ice cream cone.

And of course, the human gene.

A Shocking Patent

The human gene?

How is that even possible? Could you patent a cat's whiskers? A cloud formation? A comb-over for a balding man? (Ah, well, yes, there is a comb-over patent out there somewhere.)

The idea that the essence of our biology could be patented in the manner of an alarm clock or windshield wiper, however, came as a shock to the many of us who don't follow the legal struggles of the biotech world. Yet gene patents have existed for 30 years.

Until, that is, the U.S. Supreme Court unanimously declared last week [June 2013] that the natural human gene cannot be commercially owned.

Many of us were unaware that this was even a thing until last month, when Angelina Jolie announced that she had opted for a double mastectomy after discovering she carries a genetic mutation that gave her an 87% chance of developing breast cancer and a 50% chance of ovarian cancer at some point in

The Impact of Human Gene Patent Monopolies

Because the PTO [US Patent and Trademark Office] grants patents on the [human] genes themselves, it essentially gives patent holders a monopoly over the patented genes and all of the information contained within them. Gene patent holders have the right to prevent anyone from studying, testing or even examining a gene. As a result, scientific research and genetic testing have been delayed, limited, or even shut down due to concerns about gene patents, and patients' options regarding their medical care have been restricted.

American Civil Liberties Union, May 27, 2009.

her life. She had discovered her risk after taking an expensive test developed by Myriad Genetics, the Utah firm whose gene patents were the subject of the Supreme Court decision.

"The cost of testing for BRCA1 and BRCA2, at more than $3,000 in the United States, remains an obstacle for many women," Jolie wrote in the *New York Times*.

Her mild critique unleashed a whiff of unseemliness about the cost of the BRACAnalysis test, as many women—especially the uninsured—came forward to say they were at risk but could not afford to take it.

A Biotech Monopoly

Why is the test so expensive? There's no competition; Myriad has a zealously enforced monopoly.

After Jolie's bombshell essay ran, Myriad went into something of a defensive crouch, insisting the great majority of its tests are covered by health insurance. The company said it has provided financial assistance to 5,000 women who could not afford the fee.

The very idea that a biotech company could hold a monopoly on a piece of the human genome (let alone a test) was offensive to most of us lay folks, even if the purpose was a noble one: a diagnostic test that would reveal whether a person earned a gene mutation that made her more likely to get breast or ovarian cancer.

Myriad had claimed that by isolating the genes from the rest of the human genome, it had created something outside the realm of the natural world. "No one can patent anyone's genes," the company says on its website. "In order to unravel the mysteries of what genes do, researchers have had to separate them from the rest of the DNA by producing man-made copies. . . . These man-made copies, called 'isolated DNA,' are unique chemical compositions not found in nature or the human body."

Not so, said the court, concurring with the geneticists— including a principal researcher on the Human Genome Project—who filed friend-of-the-court briefs.

"A naturally occurring DNA segment is a product of nature and not patent eligible merely because it has been isolated," wrote Justice Clarence Thomas, who wrote the court's opinion.

Nothing "man-made" about it.

The financial stakes are what make the concept worth fighting over. According to *Forbes* magazine, Myriad spent $500 million over the course of 17 years before it turned a profit on its patented BRACAnalysis test. But the payoff has come. Last year, the company's profit margin was 22.6% on revenues of nearly $500 million. More than 80% of Myriad's revenue comes from the proprietary test.

A Dark Narrative

Myriad, though, despite its groundbreaking and lifesaving work, has come off as some sort of villain in the drama.

"A company that is widely regarded as being an efficient laboratory, was a startup that helped discover the genetic cause of two dread[ed] cancers and provides a service that allows people at risk to mitigate the risk is nonetheless reviled," wrote geneticists Robert Cook-Deegan and A.L. Baldwin of Duke University last January [2012] in the journal *Genome Medicine*. "This should be a hero story, but is instead a dark narrative."

Citing a review of English-language articles about Myriad and its BRCA gene patents, the authors said that Myriad has not only received more attention than other companies involved in gene patent controversies, but that nearly 78% of the coverage was negative.

Why has Myriad ended up with a black eye? The authors say it wasn't the gene patents—lots of companies have them. But in its relentless protection of the patents, the writers said, Myriad acquired a reputation not just for "legalistic bullying" but for obstructing research. Cook-Deegan and Baldwin cited one case study of Myriad that found that to many researchers, "it seemed Myriad was willing to block scientific research to turn a profit."

Among the plaintiffs in the case against Myriad were geneticists who claimed they were forced to stop administering tests to patients, even though they charged less than half of what Myriad charged, and patients who were dismayed they were unable to get second opinions.

Myriad defends itself from those charges on its website and notes that 18,000 scientists have studied the patented genes, and 10,000 scientific papers have been published about them.

Still, it was hard to find anyone who was disappointed by the Supreme Court's ruling. Even Myriad put on a happy face, tweeting: "Now that the Supreme Court battle is over, it's back to the REAL battle—the one against disease!"

Personally, I'm thinking about patenting a four-legged pantyhose.

> *"Gene patents ... harm women who have not been able to get information about whether or not they have a mutation that increases their risk of breast and ovarian cancer."*

Human Gene Patents Hurt Women

Kim Irish

In the following viewpoint, Kim Irish claims that human gene patents hurt women in several ways. Because of the high cost of breast cancer gene mutation tests, many high-risk women cannot afford to be tested. The breast cancer gene patent monopoly also hurts women because it restricts development of tests that identify other possible mutations, particularly in women of color, Irish maintains. Moreover, gene testing monopolies limit second-opinion tests necessary for effective decision making when tests detect breast cancer gene mutations. This breast cancer gene-patent monopoly prevents lifesaving research by others, placing profit over women's health, she concludes. Irish was, at the time of this viewpoint, program manager of BCAction, a breast cancer awareness advocacy organization.

As you read, consider the following questions:

1. What does Irish claim are some of the challenges faced by insured women who want Myriad's BRACAnalysis test?

2. According to Irish, what did Myriad report for a time as its "false negative" rate?

3. What percentage of the women who die of breast cancer each year die of hereditary breast cancer, according to Irish?

Thank you for the opportunity to speak today. My name is Kimberly Irish, and I bring a different perspective to this hearing today. I represent Breast Cancer Action (or BCAction). BCAction is a national education and advocacy organization that carries the voices of women affected by breast cancer— living with and at risk of the disease—in order to inspire and compel the changes necessary to end the breast cancer epidemic. We represent over 40,000 members nationwide, some of whom have a known BRCA[1] mutation, some of whom do not know if they have a BRCA mutation, and some of whom have no known mutation. We accomplish our mission through working on our three program priorities—putting patients first, where we advocate for more effective and less toxic breast cancer treatments by shifting the balance of power in the Food and Drug Administration's drug approval process away from the pharmaceutical industry and toward the public interest, creating healthy environments, where we work to decrease involuntary environmental exposures that put people at risk for breast cancer, and eliminating social inequities, where we work to create awareness that it is not just genes, but social

---

1. BRCA genes produce proteins responsible for repairing DNA. If these genes are damaged, they cannot repair damaged DNA properly, increasing the risk of breast and ovarian cancer.

injustices that lead to disparities in breast cancer incidence and outcomes. We are also plaintiffs in the lawsuit against Myriad Genetics.[2]

Key Dangers of Gene Patents

Breast Cancer Action opposes gene patents because they harm women in five key ways:

1. They harm women who have not been able to get information about whether or not they have a mutation that increases their riskj of breast and ovarian cancer.

Some women can't get the test because of the monopoly and high cost.

The test may not look at some women's particular mutation (because even the second test combined with the first doesn't look at every possible mutation, just the common ones).

Women who had the test with an indeterminate result are also harmed, because it is not clear from this whether their risk of breast and ovarian cancer increases.

2. Women who were able to get genetic testing and have a clear result are also harmed because, as Congresswoman Wasserman-Schultz described. . . :

They should have access to independent second opinion testing before making decisions about organ-removing surgery.

3. Finally, both groups of women suffer when there are impediments to potentially life saving research.

---

2. The case was decided on June 13, 2013. In *Association for Molecular Pathology v. Myriad Genetics*, Justice Clarence Thomas, writing for a majority of the US Supreme Court, held that "A naturally occurring DNA segment is a product of nature and not patent eligible merely because it has been isolated."

By permission of Cathy Wilcox, Fairfax Media.

Not all patients are equally harmed. Sometimes things go dramatically wrong and women are unable to get the information they need. I'll talk about that. Other times, it seems that things worked as they should have when women are able to get information on their mutation. But even in these seemingly "best case" scenarios, there are important ways that gene patents harm women. Let me explain.

The Impact of a Patent Monopoly

The first reason Breast Cancer Action opposes Myriad Genetics' patents on the BRCA1 and BRCA2 genes is that the monopoly means that too many women can't access this expensive test. Myriad's monopoly also means that there is no competition present from other companies whatsoever. There are no other options for patients to choose from, so the cost remains high and out of reach for far too many women.

Because of the patents Myriad Genetics holds on these genes, the company can charge whatever it wants for testing, though other labs say they could charge far less. Make no mistake about it—genetic diagnostic testing is expensive. Myriad Genetics' BRACAnalysis test costs approximately $3,500, with the supplemental BRACAnalysis Large Rearrangement Test in High Risk Patients test (or BART) costing an additional $700. Though some health insurance companies will cover the cost (or a portion of the cost) of testing, not all companies do so. Each insurance company must negotiate with Myriad individually—and we hear stories of women, including a plaintiff in the lawsuit against Myriad, as noted earlier, whose insurance did not have a contract for services for the test. In addition, the BART test is not always covered by insurance, even if the first test is. For women without health insurance—and according to the U.S. Department of Health and Human Services, that number is more than 17 million women between the ages of 18 and 64—the test is simply not affordable. Uninsured and under-insured women deserve to have the same opportunity to access testing that women with insurance coverage have.

The Limits of Testing

Second, only some mutations are evaluated in Myriad's standard "Comprehensive BRACAnalysis." For some high-risk women, in particular women of Latin American and Hispanic ancestry, about 10% of the mutations (called large rearrangements) are missed by the standard BRACAnalysis test. Testing for large rearrangements requires a separate test that is often not covered by insurance.

A third issue is that current testing has limitations in what it can detect. That is, the two tests combined still only look at some of the possible mutations, and there are others of unknown significance. Myriad test results can be indeterminate—one study found that as many as 10% of people tested had an indeterminate test result, a disproportionate number of whom are women of color. What are women supposed to do when the results are unclear? Should they have prophylactic surgeries? Will their insurance cover increased screenings?

Inadequate Second-Opinion Testing

A fourth critical problem with Myriad's patents is that independent second-opinion testing is not widely available, if at all. And like Professor Misha Angrist from the Duke Institute for Genomic Sciences & Policy who spoke earlier, today is the first I've heard that other labs can conduct testing. So if someone tests negative or positive for BRCA gene mutations, how do they know this finding is accurate? For a time, Myriad reported that its method of testing resulted in a high false negative rate—as much as 12%. Before making life-altering decisions wouldn't YOU want to have the option of a second opinion confirming the results? Nancy S., a Breast Cancer Action member, who tested positive for the BRCA mutations, was not offered second-opinion testing by her doctor because it wasn't an option. In fact, none of BCAction's members have reported that they could access second-opinion testing, or that they even knew it was an option. Women who are at significant hereditary risk and base important screening and other decisions on negative results, or are considering life-altering prophylactic surgeries (where organs and other body parts are removed) should be able to access second-opinion testing on which to base these significant decisions. Just as women want to be able to access second opinions from doctors, it is understandable that they may want access to independent second-opinion testing as well.

Women of color (including African-American and Asian-American women) are more likely than white women to receive uncertain test results, creating many questions about which follow-up steps they should take, such as: "Does an indeterminate result warrant prophylactic surgery?" and "Does it justify increased monitoring and if so, will insurance pay for it?" Runi Limary, an Asian-American woman and plaintiff in the lawsuit challenging Myriad's patents, received ambiguous results when she had genetic testing done. Runi was told that this "variant of uncertain significance" has been seen in Asian women, and that these ambiguous results seem to come up more for women of color.

The Limits on Future Research

The fifth issue is the limits on future research that may benefit women. BCAction believes that current and future research, which has the potential to save many lives, should not be limited by Myriad Genetics' monopoly on BRCA1 and BRCA2 genes and testing. Last year over 230,000 women were diagnosed with invasive breast cancer. 40,000 women die of the disease each year. Up to 10% may be associated with hereditary risk, including known and as-yet-unknown BRCA mutations. We, our families, and our friends, cannot wait for better prevention, treatment, and surgery. Limits that inhibit other labs from doing tests and research that could save the lives of our mothers, sisters, friends, daughters, wives, and partners are simply not acceptable.

When women cannot access testing, when the test fails to provide conclusive evidence about a particular mutation, when the test provides an indeterminate result, when second-opinion testing is not accessible, and when creativity and innovation in research is limited that could potentially save lives, we all suffer. Breast Cancer Action urges an end to gene patents so that women's health comes first.

"*The Supreme Court decision in the* Myriad *case is historic, but the tension between profit and scientific freedom lives on.*"

The Supreme Court Gene-Patent Decision Will Inhibit Genetic Research

Sharon Levy

The US Supreme Court decision in Association for Molecular Pathology v. Myriad Genetics, *which held that isolated genes are a product of nature and thus not patent eligible, may inhibit genetic research, claims Sharon Levy in the following viewpoint. Some fear that the decision fails to clarify how much intervention is necessary to make a natural object a human invention, she asserts. Nor did the court clearly overturn an oft-cited decision that does not actually address the right to patent natural substances, posing a threat to pharmaceutical companies who patent natural chemicals, Levy maintains. Levy writes on ecology, evolution, and environmental science issues.*

As you read, consider the following questions:

1. According to Levy, how many gene patents may be impacted by the *Myriad* decision?

Sharon Levy, "Our Shared Code: The *Myriad* Decision and the Future of Genetic Research," *Environmental Health Perspectives*, vol. 121, no. 8, August 2013, pp. A250–253. Reproduced with permission from Environmental Health Perspectives.

2. According to agricultural economist Gregory Graff, why is the species of origin of a claimed DNA sequence not always clear?

3. According to patent attorney and science historian Jon Harkness, what was young Supreme Court Justice Learned Hand ignorant of in the oft-cited *Parke-Davis v. Mulford* decision?

Christopher Mason felt euphoric. On the morning of 13 June 2013 Mason, a geneticist at Weill Cornell Medical College in New York, had just heard news of the Supreme Court's opinion in the case *Association for Molecular Pathology et al. v. Myriad Genetics, Inc., et al.* The Court had decided that "a naturally occurring DNA segment is a product of nature and not patent eligible merely because it has been isolated."

"I was ecstatic," Mason says. "This was a huge victory for patients, scientists, and clinicians; the genome is finally free, your genes are finally yours." For 15 years Myriad's patents had given it a monopoly on *BRCA* gene testing in the United States, limiting the availability of the test and making it impossible for some patients to obtain a second opinion on their results. Concerned that gene patents put him and other researchers at risk of expensive lawsuits, Mason had worked as an expert witness in the case and coauthored a paper in *Genome Medicine* exploring the ways in which patents like Myriad's clashed with basic concepts in genetics and could stifle genetic research.

After the June [2013] ruling, many news outlets reported that the Supreme Court had ruled that "human genes cannot be patented." But much of the coverage missed the ambiguity in the decision and the divide between legal doctrine and scientific understanding reflected in the case. And although the Court's decision settled some vexing problems, many questions remain.

Myriad's Patent Claims

The first U.S. gene patent was granted in 1982. Since then, researchers have estimated that patents had been granted covering 20% to 41% of the human genome. And while the exact number of extant gene patents prior to the June 2013 ruling is unknown, they have been estimated to number in the thousands. However, University of Missouri–Kansas City law professor Christopher Holman says these studies overestimated the number of patent claims by counting patents that merely refer to gene sequences without asserting claims to them. (A claim is the portion of the patent that lays out exactly what the patent is intended to protect.)

The focus of the Supreme Court case was Myriad's patents on isolated forms of the genes BRCA1 and BRCA2, which its scientists had co-discovered in the early 1990s. (Researchers at the National Institutes of Health were also involved in the discovery of BRCA1.) These genes are associated with an increased risk of breast and ovarian cancer. Under Myriad's patents, no other U.S. laboratory could test for these DNA sequences without risking a patent infringement lawsuit.

Myriad's patents included some particularly far-reaching claims. Claims 5 and 6 asserted rights not only to the complete BRCA genes, but also to segments as short as 15 base pairs ("mers") in length. Because nucleotide patterns repeat many times within the human genome—and, for that matter, in the genomes of other species—these claims, if enforced, would have allowed Myriad to block a wide range of research and clinical testing. Human chromosome 1, for instance, contains more than 300,000 oligonucleotides covered by the 15-mer claim on BRCA1.

Because Myriad enforced its patents against competitors in clinical testing, it became the focus of a lawsuit brought by the American Civil Liberties Union (ACLU) and the Public Patent Foundation on behalf of patients, medical providers, and professional organizations, including the Association for Molecular Pathology.

In taking on the Myriad case, the Supreme Court agreed to consider the question of whether human genes could be patented—adopting the phrasing used by the ACLU in its complaint. Gregory Graff, an agricultural economist at Colorado State University, was lead author on a recent paper in *Nature Biotechnology* that warned of the potential tangle that could result from a ruling that applied only to human genes. Like Mason, he pointed out that although the Court had agreed to consider the question of whether human genes can be patented, the biological reality is that DNA is just DNA; the human genetic code is not much different from that of many other life forms.

Graff's analysis found that valid patents claimed isolated DNA more often from plants, animals, and microbes than from the human genome. But gene sequences from many other species overlap with sections of the human genome, and given how patents are written, Graff says, the species of origin of a claimed DNA sequence is not always clear.

Striking a Balance

The justices solved this problem by making no mention of "human" versus "nonhuman" DNA in their decision and ruled simply that naturally occurring DNA sequences are ineligible to be patented; this settles the concerns of many critics. But the Court also held that complementary DNA (cDNA) can be patented because it does not occur in nature—it is a transcript of natural protein-encoding DNA sequences from which noncoding sequences called introns have been removed. Because cDNA is synthesized and used constantly in genomic research and in pharmaceutical production, the ramifications of this decision for future studies are unclear.

"The opinion is not terribly coherent," says Dan Burk, a professor of law at the University of California, Irvine, who holds degrees in molecular biology and biochemistry. "It's a short opinion that leaves a lot of questions unanswered."

The opinion, written by Justice Clarence Thomas, begins by laying out some basics of molecular biology. Thomas notes that a gene isolated in the laboratory contains the same genetic information as a gene in a living cell, and concludes that isolated genes are therefore products of nature and not patent eligible. But cDNA, which is transcribed in the laboratory from messenger RNA, is free of the introns found in the native genome. cDNA sequences are useful because they carry genetic information identical to that found in nature, but that detail was deemed irrelevant.

A Longstanding Question

Burk believes this philosophical shifting of gears mid-decision shows the justices were seeking a way to limit gene patenting without undermining the numerous patents involved in the biotechnology and pharmaceutical industries. Jacob Sherkow, a fellow at Stanford University's Center for Law and the Bio-Sciences, agrees that the Court's decision frees up clinical genetic testing, which nearly always uses isolated genes.

Other processes, such as splicing human DNA into bacteria in order to mass-produce a human protein, require the use of cDNA. But Sherkow believes such patents won't present much of a practical problem. "Any clever researcher or patent agent will be able to work their way around patents on cDNAs," he says. "Add a couple nucleotides, take out one exon, manipulate the sequence a bit, and you're almost certain to fall outside of patent protection."

Bioethicist David Resnik of the National Institute of Environmental Health Sciences explains that the justices were grappling with the longstanding question of just how much human ingenuity is required to transform a natural object into an invention. He thinks the Court struck a reasonable balance. "Raw sequence data will be freely available," he says, "but significant changes to the sequence data will be protected."

A Touchstone Case

For Sherkow, the greatest significance of the Supreme Court decision is that it ends the 30-year-old practice of granting patents on isolated DNA. However, the decision could have implications that reach far beyond gene patenting if it is used to overturn the century-old legal doctrine that allows the patenting of all sorts of biological substances isolated from nature.

That doctrine rests on a 1911 decision in *Parke-Davis v. Mulford*, a dispute over a patent on the hormone adrenaline. In his decision, Judge Learned Hand, who was then just beginning his career on the bench, allowed the patent to stand and declared that useful substances newly isolated from nature were patentable. By the end of his life, Hand would be considered an outstanding jurist, especially revered for his rulings on patents and intellectual property. In 1958 attorneys used his decision in the *Parke-Davis* case to successfully argue for their client's right to patent vitamin B_{12}.

Following the success of the claim on vitamin B_{12}, Hand's decision in *Parke-Davis* would become a touchstone for generations of patent lawyers. It was cited in the U.S. Patent and Trade Office guidelines issued in 2001. In early rounds of the *Myriad* lawsuit, the company's attorneys cited Hand's ruling as a crucial precedent.

That changed in 2012, after Jon Harkness, a patent attorney and a science historian at the University of Minnesota, dug through original documents in the National Archives to examine the history of the *Parke-Davis* case. He discovered that the attorneys in the case had never argued the merits of patent rights on biological substances. Learned Hand listened to a dispute over who had priority rights to the patent, not an analysis of whether molecules found in nature should be patented at all. When he stated that an isolated hormone could be patented, he was ignorant of an important Patent Office precedent established in 1889, which disallowed a patent for

The Bermuda Principles

One of the early principles agreed upon by leaders of the Human Genome Project was that the DNA sequence generated should be freely available to the public. This principle was codified in the 1997 Bermuda Principles, which set forth the expectation that all DNA sequence information should be released into publicly available databases within 24 hours of being generated. This policy of open access to the genome has been a core ethos of genomics ever since.

National Human Genome Research Institute, June 19, 2013.

the fibrous core extracted from pine needles on the grounds that the claimant had invented nothing and was simply using an object that exists in nature.

Harkness summed up this history in a 2011 article. "If the U.S. Supreme Court agrees to consider *Myriad*," he wrote, "the justices should not turn to *Parke-Davis* for sage guidance from a judicial genius. Instead, they need to grapple with a difficult question that arises from this old case: Has the time come to reverse the trajectory of historical inertia that began with a small—almost inadvertent—shove in the wrong direction, a century ago, from an inexperienced and under-informed district court judge?" Soon after the article was published, Harkness notes, Myriad's attorneys stopped mentioning *Parke-Davis* as a precedent.

Correcting Past Mistakes

Harkness now believes the Supreme Court decision in *Myriad* has corrected Learned Hand's century-old mistake. Sherkow would welcome the demise of the *Parke-Davis* doctrine, but he isn't sure that it's done for; the wording of the ruling suggests, but never clearly states, that Hand's *Parke-Davis* decision is defunct as a precedent. Just what this means in terms of future efforts to patent isolated molecules other than DNA is unclear.

"The impact of this decision could reverberate beyond genetic medicine," says Harkness. "It might mean that chemicals found in plants or microbes—which are the sources of many pharmaceuticals—can no longer be patented."

Resnik is concerned that doing away with patents on isolated molecules would be detrimental to the pharmaceutical, chemical, and biotechnology industries. He hopes that's not how the Supreme Court decision will be interpreted. "Myriad's patent claims applied to the information contained in the chemical structure of DNA, not to the exact chemical formula of the structure itself," he says. "One could hold that you can't patent information, i.e., sequence data, but you can patent chemical structures that you have isolated and purified."

Proprietary Data

Myriad's patent-authorized monopoly on *BRCA* gene testing may have ended, but its legacy will continue. Beginning in late 2004 the company chose to withhold information on variations of the *BRCA* gene from public databases. "Myriad has more data on *BRCA* mutations than anyone else," explains Robert Cook-Deegan, a research professor in the Institute for Genome Sciences and Policy and the Sanford School of Public Policy at Duke University. He fears that proprietary databases like Myriad's could hinder the progress of genetic medicine. "Databases and trade secrets," he notes, "don't expire like patents do."

In most cases, *BRCA* analysis clearly shows whether an individual is at increased risk of breast and ovarian cancer. But some patients' *BRCA* genes possess what are called "variants of unknown significance" (VUS). In such cases, deciding whether a patient is at elevated cancer risk is a tough call. Because it has access to information on rare *BRCA* variants in its proprietary database, Myriad claims that only 3% of its analyses are returned with a diagnosis of VUS, as opposed to about 20% for most European laboratories.

Myriad has recently expanded its business into Germany, Switzerland, France, Italy, and Spain. The company claims it can offer a better standard of *BRCA* testing than any European lab thanks to the information in its proprietary database.

Because those data are held as a trade secret, Myriad's analyses of different *BRCA* mutations have not received clinical peer review; to protect the company's trade secret, the company expects medical providers and patients to take its conclusions on faith. In the United States, Myriad has agreements with numerous health plans that have accepted those terms. Cook-Deegan hopes European health plans and providers will push Myriad to share its data—perhaps by refusing to cover its tests until the data are made public.

Cook-Deegan acknowledges that the value of Myriad's database will dissipate with time, as other labs compile data on *BRCA* variations. But he points out that the information should belong to the patients from whom it was gathered, not to Myriad. A group of medical professionals have launched an effort to reconstruct Myriad's database by crowdsourcing data—having patients submit the results they obtain from Myriad to a public database.

An Uneasy Bargain

Patents are meant to serve as a bargain between inventors and the public: The workings of the invention are disclosed in the patent, and in return, the inventor gets 20 years of exclusive rights to his idea. The theory is that patent rights ultimately make scientists more willing to share their useful results. But that's not how things have worked out in the case of Myriad and *BRCA*, according to Cook-Deegan. "Here's a case where patents are giving rise to a huge body of trade secrets," he notes. "The patent system is not a solution to trade secrecy in the case of genetic diagnostics. It looks like it's the cause of the problem."

That matters in the aftermath of the *Myriad* decision, because other nations, including Australia and members of the European Union, still allow patents on isolated DNA. Myriad is one of only three companies that refuse to share their information in public databases, but in this case, Cook-Deegan fears that the actions of a single corporation may cause a bottleneck in the progress of genetic medicine. The Supreme Court decision in the *Myriad* case is historic, but the tension between profit and scientific freedom lives on.

"*The Supreme Court wisely held back from a premature ruling which could inhibit future research and development . . . which inevitably is both lengthy and costly to undertake.*"

The Supreme Court Gene-Patent Decision Will Not Inhibit Genetic Research

Ed Mannino

In the following viewpoint, Ed Mannino asserts that the US Supreme Court decision in Association for Molecular Pathology v. Myriad Genetics *will not inhibit research. The Court was, in fact, concerned with how best to promote innovation while also discouraging broad patents that inhibit competition, he asserts. Thus, the Court did not decide whether the manipulation of genes, new applications based on genetic knowledge, or genetic alterations would be patentable. Indeed, the Court decided that while a naturally occurring DNA segment was not patent eligible, synthetic DNA (cDNA) would be eligible, he claims. Ed Mannino, a trial lawyer and historian, is author of* Shaping America: The Supreme Court and American Society.

As you read, consider the following questions:

1. On what section of the Patent Act did the Court rely?

2. Why does cDNA not face the same obstacles as naturally occurring DNA segments?

3. What part of the opinion do critics of the decision neglect, in the author's view?

In its much-anticipated opinion on the patenting of human genes, the Supreme Court decided to split the baby.[1] In *Association for Molecular Pathology v. Myriad Genetics, Inc.*, No. 12-398 (June 13, 2013), a unanimous court ruled that a naturally occurring DNA segment was not patent eligible, but synthetic or complementary (composite) DNA (cDNA) was.

Determining What Is Patentable

The case before the court involved patents which were granted on both DNA and cDNA. Myriad Genetics, the patentee, had discovered the exact location and sequence of two genes, mutations which had the capacity to significantly increase the risk of developing breast and ovarian cancer. Several patents were granted on both isolated DNA and synthetic DNA.

In ruling that the isolated DNA was not patent eligible, Justice Thomas' opinion for eight members of the court relied upon section 101 of the Patent Act, which requires an invention or discovery to be "new and useful." The court pointed out that there is a judicially-created exception providing that "Laws of nature, natural phenomenon and abstract ideas are not patentable" under this section, because "without this exception, there would be considerable danger that the grant of patents would 'tie up' the use of such tools and thereby 'in-

---

1. To split the baby refers to a Biblical story in which King Solomon of Israel tricked two women both claiming to be the mother of a child into revealing their true feelings by threatening to cut the baby in half. In legal jargon, it means to compromise by dividing damage awards or placing blame equally on both parties.

hibit future innovation premised upon them.'" This is so even when the discoveries at issue, including those made by Myriad Genetics, were "[g]roundbreaking, innovative or even brilliant," and even when extensive research efforts were required to locate and isolate the genes.

With respect to naturally occurring DNA, "Myriad did not create anything," so the patent on that DNA was improperly granted.

By contrast, "cDNA does not present the same obstacles to patentability as naturally occurring, isolated DNA segments." This is so because a cDNA segment is created, rather than naturally occurring. Indeed, even if the sequence at issue is "dictated by nature," nevertheless "the lab technician unquestionably creates something new when cDNA is made." As such, if all of the other requirements for patentability were satisfied, the patents granted "would . . . give Myriad the exclusive right to synthetically create BRCA cDNA."

On this issue, the court significantly cautioned in footnote 9 that "We express no opinion whether cDNA satisfies the other statutory requirements of patentability." These include such requirements as the novelty and non-obviousness of the invention. Thus, those who criticize the decision as granting patents on subject matter that is obvious neglect this part of the majority opinion, and the comment in that opinion regarding the sequence being "dictated by nature" could make the cDNA claims subject to attack under section 103, a point the court did not reach.

Addressing Polar Fears

As we noted in our April 16 [2013] post on the oral argument in this case, many of the justices were concerned with rendering a broad decision on the patentability of human genes because of the polar fears of inhibiting competition by granting broad patents, on the one hand, and of discouraging innovation by denying patents on new discoveries, on the other hand. Thus in addition to not deciding the question of whether cDNA met the other requirements for obtaining a patent, the majority opinion in its final substantive paragraph specifically stated that "It is important to note what is not implicated by this decision." First, since no method claims relating to DNA were before the court, the question of whether a method patent could be granted on some aspect of "manipulating genes" was not ruled out. Second, the opinion did not cover patents on "new applications of knowledge" about genes, and indeed several unchallenged claims in Myriad's patents were limited to such applications. Third, the court declined to decide whether DNA could be patented where "the order of the naturally occurring nucleotides has been altered." In sum, the Supreme Court made clear that it was "merely" holding that "genes and the information they encode are not patent eligible under [section] 101 simply because they have been isolated from the surrounding genetic material."

By carefully limiting the scope of its opinion to a single ground of patent eligibility, and by specifically leaving open the possibility of obtaining patents on (1) methods of manipulating genes, (2) applications of knowledge regarding human genes, or (3) alterations of genetic codes, the Supreme Court wisely held back from a premature ruling which could inhibit future research and development in this area, which inevitably is both lengthy and costly to undertake.

Periodical and Internet Sources Bibliography

The following articles have been selected to supplement the diverse views presented in this chapter.

Ronald Bailey	"Should We Patent Human Genes?" *Reason*, June 12, 2013.
Emily Bazelon	"Patently Unfair," *Slate*, June 13, 2013.
Marcy Darnovsky and Karuna Jaggar	"Who Should Own DNA? All of Us," *Los Angeles Times*, April 12, 2013.
Charles Davis	"The More One Shares, the More One Undermines a Future Patent Application and a System That Encourages Privatisation," *Al Jazeera*, August 3, 2013.
Kenneth Jost	"Patenting Human Genes," *CQ Researcher*, May 31, 2013.
Nicole D. Kling	"The Supreme Court on Myriad: Will It Stifle Innovation?" KevinMD.com, July 26, 2013.
Peter D. Meldrum	"Myriad Genetics: Patents Save Lives, Aid Innovation," *USA Today*, April 14, 2013.
Andrew Pollack	"After Patent Ruling, Availability of Gene Test Could Broaden," *New York Times*, June 13, 2013.
Jacob S. Sherkow and Henry T. Greely	"The Future of Gene Patents and the Implications for Medicine," *JAMA Internal Medicine*, July 29, 2013.
Susan Young	"U.S. Supreme Court Says 'Natural' Human Genes May Not Be Patented," *MIT Technology Review*, June 13, 2013.

Are Human Genetic Tests Beneficial?

Chapter Preface

Although some genetic testing companies claim that they can identify genetic links to high-risk diseases or poor drug responses, according to Jeffrey Shuren, director, Center for Devices and Radiological Health at the Food and Drug Administration, in many cases this link has not been well established by research. Thus, he claims, in some cases genetic testing information puts consumers at risk of making poor health decisions. In truth, research reveals that most diseases have multiple genetic and environmental causes. Moreover, some question the accuracy of many genetic tests. A 2010 study at the Cleveland Clinic's Genomic Medicine Institute reported that family medical histories turned up a greater number of people at high risk for colon cancer than did a direct-to-consumer test. The inaccuracy of tests and a lack of knowledge about what exactly the results mean are, in fact, of concern to many. Thus, some critics express concern when college students and student athletes are invited or required to submit DNA for testing. Indeed, one of several controversies in the genetic testing debate is whether such programs are appropriate or useful.

The University of California, Berkeley, invited freshman and transfer students to send genetic samples for testing. The tests would identify genetic markers for the ability to metabolize alcohol, break down lactose, and absorb folates (B vitamins). After school began, these students could see their results and attend optional lectures on genetic testing. Jeremy Gruber, president of the Council for Responsible Genetics, thought the program was inappropriate. "To be so cavalier about using genetic testing in this way without appropriate safeguards is really astonishing and a very large disservice to the students they're supposed to be educating,"[1] he wrote.

1. Quoted in Victoria Colliver, "Ethics of UC Berkeley's Gene Testing Questioned," *San Francisco Chronicle*, May 21, 2010.

Center for Genetics and Society policy analyst Jesse Reynolds agreed that the program was ill-advised, citing challenges to commercial direct-to-consumer testing. "Just last week [May 2010], the largest drugstore in the country [Walgreens] halted plans to retail a similar product after receiving a stern letter from the U.S. Food and Drug Administration," Reynolds asserts. "If selling genetic tests directly to consumers is a problem in the eyes of the federal government, how can the university justify pushing them on thousands of 18-year-olds?"[2]

In response to critics, University officials argued that the program was voluntary, and the samples were tested for innocuous conditions not serious diseases such as colon and breast cancer. Moreover, school officials assured critics that they would vigorously maintain student privacy. "What we hoped to do is expose our students to the science behind personalized medicine and engage them in the discussion about what the future may hold,"[3] argued Mark Schlissel, UC Berkeley's dean of biological sciences and immunology. "We could have sent all the students a magazine article or book to read, but we thought it would be far more engaging to actually involve in them in a genetic test."[4]

Another controversial issue is a 2010 National Collegiate Athletic Association (NCAA) policy that requires all Division 1 college athletes [to] be genetically screened for sickle cell anemia. This blood disorder, especially common among people of sub-Saharan African descent, can lead to death after intense exercise, even among those who show no symptoms of the disease. Death related to exercise can be 10 to 30 times higher among those with the genetic mutation. The NCAA's policy was part of a legal settlement over the death of 19-year-old Dale Lloyd, then a freshman at Rice University. Lloyd, who did not know he had the sickle cell trait, died following football practice. Critics claim that the well-intentioned policy is

2. *Ibid.*
3. *Ibid.*
4. *Ibid.*

inadequate. According to Johns Hopkins Medicine, the policy fails to address the problem of false-positive test results, which often occur in genetics tests. Moreover, they argue, the policy does not provide adequate counseling to help students understand the difference between carrying the gene and having the disease. Others fear these students might be unfairly banned from athletics. Dr. Lanetta Jordan, the chief medical officer for the Sickle Cell Disease Association of America asks, "Does it now slide from protection of the athlete who has S.C.T. [sickle cell trait] by sitting them out, to maybe losing a scholarship, to maybe not being recruited at all?"[5] Still other commentators claim that the test does little to make practice safer when heat and humidity are high. "There's not any data that shows that screening can save lives," argues Dr. William Roberts, who coedited a set of recommendations by six medical organizations on preseason physicals. "A lot of the kids who have died, they've known they have sickle-cell trait and they still run them to death. It should just be a change in the training program to protect everyone and not just the kids with sickle."[6]

Whether optional or mandatory genetic testing of students or student athletes is appropriate remains hotly contested. The authors in the following chapter express their views on other controversies in answer to the question: Are human genetic tests beneficial? Balancing the risks and benefits of genetic testing continues to challenge all stakeholders.

---

5. Quoted in Katie Thomas and Brett Zarda, "In N.C.A.A., Question of Bias Over a Test for a Genetic Trait," *New York Times*, April 11, 2010.
6. *Ibid.*

> *"Much [direct-to-consumer] genetic test-*
> *ing is not exceedingly reliable and not*
> *always trustworthy in terms of what it*
> *means."*

Get Ready for the Risks of Genetic Testing

Arthur Caplan

Direct-to-consumer genetic tests pose significant risks to consum-
ers argues Arthur Caplan in the following viewpoint. Many
companies do not offer genetic counseling, he maintains, and
without it, consumers may not know how to cope with the re-
sults, particularly negative ones. Moreover, the results are often
inaccurate or of little use. In fact, both genes and lifestyle deter-
mine one's health. Furthermore, Caplan concludes, companies
cannot guarantee genetic privacy. Caplan is professor and direc-
tor of the Division of Bioethics at New York University Langone
Medical Center.

As you read, consider the following questions:

1. What questions does Caplan ask of those who might
   receive direct-to-consumer genetics tests that show a
   huge risk of a fatal disease?

2. What does Caplan think of the study about consumer responses to genetic test results sponsored by 23andMe?

3. How do genes differ in terms of the percentage of certainty that a consumer will contract a disease?

Would you want to know your future if science could tell it to you?

Some forms of commercial genetic testing promise something like this kind of future-telling. But you need to think long and hard about peeking into your own genes to see what they hold in store for your health. It may not be so easy to cope with the bad news that could result. And it is likely that other people could know your genetic future even if you do not consent to tell them.

Responses to Negative Results

Let's say you send your spit (yes, spit is the source of DNA for this kind of testing) off to one of the many companies advertising direct-to-consumer genetic testing and the results showed you had a huge risk of a fatal disease.

Would that freak you out? Would you want to get this news in a letter sent by overnight mail? Wouldn't you prefer to have someone available to counsel you about what negative findings mean and what to do about them?

There are people who say they don't need help dealing with whatever the genetic tests reveal. And a new study sponsored by one of the genetic testing companies, 23andMe, backs them up—sort of. The study suggests most people can get bad news about their risk of getting or transmitting breast cancer to a new generation without going all to pieces emotionally.

I think the study is weak. It involved only a few hundred people who already likely knew they were in a high risk group for breast cancer. It is likely that such people who seek testing will take bad news with greater calm than would you or I if we had no expectations.

At most, the study suggests that people in high risk groups who know they are likely to get a genetic disease can handle negative health information. But it doesn't tell us much about how the average person will cope in such a situation.

Varied Accuracy

Remember that genetic testing is still in its infancy.

While some commercial companies promise to tell you what is the optimal diet for you to eat or whether your kid will be a star athlete, the reality is that genetic testing is nowhere near capable of doing any such thing. The accuracy of testing depends on the disease.

Some genes when present mean 100% certainty that you will get a disease, but some raise your risk only 5%. And test predictions are based on studies of small, mainly white, American populations. Testing quality depends on the lab and that is all over the place right now. So much genetic testing is not exceedingly reliable and not always trustworthy in terms of what it means for you.

Nonetheless, finding out about health risks hidden in your genes still seems to me the kind of news that at least requires you make available a trained genetic counselor to help you deal with it.

Remember genetic testing is about risk and probabilities— and the future is shaped by your genes and your lifestyle— facts that counselors can help make clear. It is cheaper for companies not to have to offer counseling. But cheaper is not necessarily better if the test comes up snake eyes for high risk for Alzheimer's, Huntington's, diabetes, cancer, depression or blindness for you or your children.

Privacy Concerns

Even if you think you have what it takes to absorb unexpectedly distressing results about your health without the help of

The Risk of Direct-to-Consumer Tests

Marketing genetic tests directly to consumers can increase the risk of a test because a patient may make a decision that adversely affects their health, such as stopping or changing the dose of a medication or continuing an unhealthy lifestyle, without the intervention of a learned intermediary. The risk points up the importance of ensuring that consumers are also provided accurate, complete, and understandable information about the limitations of test results they are obtaining.

Jeffrey Shuren,
Testimony Before US House of Representatives,
July 22, 2010.

a counselor or doctor, there is another reason to be wary of sending off your spit to a company touting affordable genetic testing on the Internet.

In January [2013], a team of American and Israeli scientists showed they could reconstruct the identity of people from supposedly anonymous genetic samples using readily available databases on the Internet. Genetic hackers who get a sample of your DNA could use public databases to figure out whose genetic sample they have and then they would know all about the future written in your genes too.

Maybe people are more resilient than worrywarts like me when it comes to facing potentially upsetting revelation about their genes. Still, it does not take a lot of people actually breaking down and crying to think that competent personal counseling always ought to be an option before finding out about your genetic destiny. And given the problems inherent in guaranteeing personal privacy when it comes to cracking your genetic code, you need to be very careful where and to whom you send your DNA.

Genetic testing is a very useful new tool for helping us stay healthy. But doctors, counselors and even legislators need to get involved so that genetic knowledge can be properly understood and kept private.

"Concerns over [direct-to-consumer] genetic testing are often disproportionate to the reality."

Direct-to-Consumer Genetic Test Concerns Are Unfounded

Ricki Lewis

Most fears about direct-to-consumer testing are unfounded, claims Ricki Lewis in the following viewpoint. Many consumers are not worried about privacy and share the risks of diseases such as breast cancer with relatives, she maintains. In fact, despite fears that the results would give little for consumers to act on, many are changing their diets, exercising more, and seeking additional information from health care professionals. Although physicians are often ill-equipped to help their patients interpret the results, efforts to bridge the knowledge gap are underway, she concludes. Lewis, a geneticist, provides genetic counseling and teaches genetic ethics at the Alden March Bioethics Institute of Albany Medical Center.

As you read, consider the following questions:

1. What did bioethicists and social scientists begin to do once direct-to-consumer testing became more popular, according to Lewis?

Ricki Lewis, "Direct-to-Consumer Genetic Testing: A New View," *DNA Science Blog,* November 8, 2012. Copyright © 2012 by PLOS and DNA Science Blog. Licensed under Creative Commons Attribution 3.0 Unported License. Reproduced by permission.

2. What was 23andMe able to do faster than would have been possible in academic medicine, in Lewis' view?

3. In Lewis' opinion, why does the public sometimes expect too much of physicians?

On a Thursday night in October 2007, I sat with hundreds of geneticists at the *American Society of Human Genetics* annual meeting in San Diego, so stunned that we ignored the free dessert. At a table in front of the crowd were several very nicely-dressed physicians and genetic counselors representing a trio of companies gearing up to offer, in the coming year, direct-to-consumer (DTC) genetic testing.

Yes, ordinary people would be able to send samples of themselves—spit, it would turn out—to companies that would charge fees to return results right to them, circumventing health care professionals. The companies had names much catchier than those of the biotech companies of the past two decades: 23andMe, Navigenics Inc. (absorbed into Life Technologies Corp last summer [2011]), and deCODE Genetics, part of Icelandic biobank fame.

We were collectively shocked, and in retrospect, I'm not sure why. But the chatter in the hallways and elevators afterwards, according to my unscientific survey and memory, was decidedly negative.

A New View

What a difference half a decade makes.

I'm at this year's [2012] annual meeting of the *American Society of Human Genetics*, where another panel of DTC genetic testing company reps are fielding questions. But this time, the audience is asking about expanding DTC services to more diverse communities.

What's changed? The DTC companies have proven their value.

After the first DTC testing companies began offering their services in April 2008, the media took notice. It was a great story. For me, the lowpoint of the derision was the *New Yorker's* Talk of the Town piece extolling the hilarity of "spit parties."

The popularity of the testing grew. A cottage industry of sorts arose as bioethicists and social scientists soon began to survey customers and dissect their characteristics, motivations, and use of the information.

For example, [the] median age of the DTC genetic test consumer is [in] the 40s. My interpretation: once people have settled down a bit, moved out of their parents' homes, gotten jobs, maybe have kids in school but not yet college, they naturally start to think about how they will kick the bucket. And here were companies offering to look into a genetic crystal ball, without even the need to bleed.

Geneticists, much more familiar with human decrepitude, had more serious concerns about testing put directly in the hands of potential patients. But doubts have been fading. "Concerns over genetic testing are often disproportionate to the reality," Tanya Moreno, PhD, Director of Research and Development at Pathway Genomics, said on the panel today [November 8, 2012].

Fears and Realities

Here are a few of those initial fears, and the realities that have come to pass:

Fear: Customers' private genetic information would be compromised.

Reality: People are blogging, tweeting, emailing, and facebooking their intimate genetic information with abandon.

Sandra S-J Lee, PhD, Senior Research Scholar from the Stanford Center for Biomedical Ethics, spoke about a survey of 80 23andMe customers that probed social networking and personal genomics. They did phone interviews, surveys, and focus groups. Nearly half of them had announced their results on Facebook, and more than 2/3 had gone online to find another person with a shared condition—and that was from 2009, when fewer of us were permanently attached to our devices.

Fear: DTC customers will focus on stupid stuff, like earwax consistency and bitter taste.

Reality: 23andMe assembled 3,426 cases and 29,624 controls to track down two new genes that contribute to Parkinson's disease, much faster than would have been possible in academic medicine. That's hardly frivolous. It's crowdsourcing science, and although a self-selected sample, it works.

Fear: Customers won't know enough or be afraid to share important information with relatives who may be affected by a discovery.

Reality: Customers learning they have a mutation in the *BRCA1* or *BRCA2* cancer risk genes indeed told their relatives. "One of the most surprising things was the extent to which people shared the information with both male and female family members. And there was a lack of extreme anxiety," shared Joanna Mountain, PhD, Senior Director of Research at 23andMe.

Fear: Customers would have to pay outrageous fees.

Reality: The opposite has happened. My student L.W. took the 23andMe test for the 3 most common *BRCA1* and *BRCA2* mutations shortly after her mother was diagnosed with breast cancer. 23andMe's test told L.W. she hadn't inherited her mother's mutation—and also that she's of Ashkenazi Jewish ancestry, something that her parents had hidden. And she spent about $100—not the $3400 that Myriad Genetics charges to sequence the genes. L.W. and her mom contributed their DNA to the Parkinson's disease project.

Bridging the Knowledge Gap

Fear: Physicians don't know enough to interpret many new genetic tests.

Reality: That's still somewhat true, for some physicians who rarely encounter genetic conditions or need to explain them. David Kaufman, PhD, Director of Research and Statistics at the Genetics and Public Policy Center at Johns Hopkins University, reported on a survey of 1,046 customers of 23andMe, Navigenics, and deCODE, conducted from January through May 2010. The top three reasons to take the tests were curiosity (94%), to learn about future diseases (91%), and to learn about ancestry (90%). Choosing DTC genetic testing following doctor recommendation was at the bottom of the list (7%).

Communication is a big part of providing care for a patient with an elevated risk of developing a genetic disease. Disconnects happen. "In one case a physician rated himself as doing an excellent job of explaining results. But the family was completely blown away. They didn't understand anything," said Cinnamon Bloss, PhD, Director of Social Sciences at the Scripps Translational Science Institute in La Jolla.

Perhaps the public expects too much because they confuse physicians and scientists, especially because some professionals are indeed both. The equating of "doctor" with "scientist" possibly dates to physician Dana Scully on the *X-Files* constantly calling herself a scientist.

"As a group doctors lack requisite knowledge in genomic medicine. Educational efforts are underway to bridge this gap," Dr. Bloss said, perhaps referring to the first Master of Science in Genomic Medicine offered at the Miller School of Medicine at the University of Miami.

Fear: The information from DTC genetic testing won't be "actionable."

Reality: Dr. Kaufman's survey of satisfied DTC customers found that 34% adopted a more healthful diet, 16% changed a drug or supplement, and 14% exercise more. Plus, 43% sought additional information on at least one tested condition, 28%

discussed findings with a health care professional, and 9% followed up with additional lab tests.

Fear: The companies will take advantage of their customers.

Reality: "We're thinking differently about the people who take part in research. We're moving from calling them 'human subjects' to considering them to be collaborators and participants in research," said Dr. Mountain.

23andMe regularly updates their participants on research findings pertinent to test results, pursues suggestions for new tests from the customers (such as sexual orientation), and publishes articles with participants in open access journals.

With consumers on board, scientists seeming to have accepted DTC testing, and doctors having to keep up with their patients who come in with test results, I think DTC genetic testing is here to stay—and poised to explode with exome and genome sequencing.

> *"You might learn some interesting-to-know facts, but [a direct-to-consumer DNA test] probably won't have any real impact on your health."*

Genetic Tests Are Not Yet Reliable or Useful

Harriet Hall

In the following viewpoint, Harriet Hall argues that direct-to-consumer tests are incomplete, often inaccurate, and, therefore, of little use for managing health. For example, most tests sample only a small portion of DNA and often do not test for serious concerns such as breast cancer. Moreover, tests only indicate the risk of getting a disease, which, in many cases, is influenced by environmental factors such as lifestyle. In addition, she claims, testing companies are not regulated and often provide health counseling services that they are not qualified to provide. Hall is a retired family physician who writes about medicine, science, and quackery.

As you read, consider the following questions:

1. What did futurist Ray Kurzweil predict when the Human Genome Project completed the sequencing of human DNA?

Harriet Hall, "Genomic Testing—Are We There Yet?," *Skeptic Magazine*, vol. 16, no. 1, 2010, pp. 4–5. Copyright © 2010 by Skeptic Magazine. All rights reserved. Reproduced by permission.

2. How many proteins does one gene in the brain produce?

3. What was a positive pharmacogenetics outcome for an acute lymphocytic leukemia patient?

Ten years ago the Human Genome Project reported the complete sequencing of human DNA, one of the greatest accomplishments of modern science. Having a map of our genome opens the door to exciting new possibilities for medical research and personalized medicine. Futurist Ray Kurzweil predicted "Genomics testing may soon be able to predict precisely what foods are best for us, prescribe individualized exercise and other lifestyle prescriptions, and recommend a personalized list of supplements, neutraceuticals [sic], and prescription drugs for maximum health and disease avoidance."

How far have we progressed towards those goals after a decade? People keep asking, like the kids in the back seat, "Are we there yet?" Many enthusiasts think that we are, and direct-to-consumer genomic testing is becoming increasingly popular.

A Personal Testing Story

In *The Language of Life: DNA and the Revolution in Personalized Medicine*, Francis S. Collins describes his experience with personal DNA testing. He submitted samples to all three of the major labs (23andMe, Navigenics, and deCODE) to see if their results would agree. Each lab tested for a different panel of gene variants although there was a lot of overlap. To assess prostate cancer risk the different companies tested for 5, 13, and 9 variants respectively, but no company tested for all 16 variants known to be related to increased risk. One company told Collins his risk of prostate cancer was average; another told him his risk was 40% higher than average. Even when testing the same variants, their interpretations varied. Variants associated with sensitivity to the drug Coumadin were rated by one company as indicating average sensitivity and by another as showing usually high sensitivity. One result highlighted the unreliability of these tests: Collins' genes predicted that his eyes were brown. They are blue.

These tests only sample less than 1/10th of 1% of your DNA. They don't test for some of the most significant variants like the BRCA1 gene of familial breast cancer. They don't ask about family history or test specifically for diseases that run in your family. They don't really know whether the high-risk gene variants cause disease: all they know is that a variant was statistically associated with a disease in a population they tested to provide a basis for comparison. Correlation doesn't mean causation. We don't know whether the risk from one gene variant is modified by the effects of other genes. The testing was done in northern European populations, so we don't know if the results are valid for other ethnic groups. And any predictions the tests currently make will be altered by new data that are constantly coming in.

So yes, the labs were accurate in identifying genetic variants, but we don't know how accurately the variants predict risk, and the risk information may not be useful. Does it do any good to know you have an increased risk of Parkinson's disease if there is no action you can take to reduce your risk?

Even if preventive actions are possible, do we really need the results of individual tests to persuade us to take those actions? Collins' tests showed that his risk of diabetes was 29% versus the average risk of 23%. He claims that was enough to change his motivation and persuade him to adopt a healthier lifestyle. One could argue that the 23% average risk should be enough to encourage all of us to adopt a healthier lifestyle: even those who might be at lower than average risk are still at some nontrivial risk and should consider prevention.

Nearly all human illnesses may be due to an interaction of hereditary and environmental factors. It will be very difficult to tease out the various contributions. Parkinson's disease can be entirely genetic in the case of certain familial mutations, or entirely environmental as in the case of poisoning with MPTP. Or it can be anywhere in between. We tend to think of one gene/one effect, but the reality is far more complex. We have only 20,000 genes. They code for an incredibly complex human body. One gene in the brain is known to make 38,000 different proteins. Genes interact to enhance or suppress each other's expressions in very complex ways.

Diabetes is 50% hereditary but only 10% of the inherited genes have been discovered. There could be many other variants each contributing only a small amount of risk, there could be rare variants with large effects, and it could be a matter of copy number variants where a section of DNA is repeated.

Doctors get frustrated when patients bring in printouts of genome-based risk estimates. Relative risks are frequently on the order of 1.5 or lower, with little power to predict who will actually develop the disease and with no real implications for management. Patients who test negative may be falsely reassured and thus less motivated to comply with preventive recommendations. Doctors have to tell patients the printouts don't mean much: family history and general preventive advice are probably more important.

Laboratory Regulation/Reliability

The laboratories offering these tests are not regulated by the FDA [US Food and Drug Administration] but come under state jurisdiction. They have faced legal challenges. The California Department of Public Health sent "cease and desist" letters to 13 companies in 2008. New York State sent 31 letters to companies, saying they will require licenses to solicit DNA specimens from state residents. The FTC is investigating possibly deceptive advertising and marketing. Legal experts are arguing about whether giving patients information about their

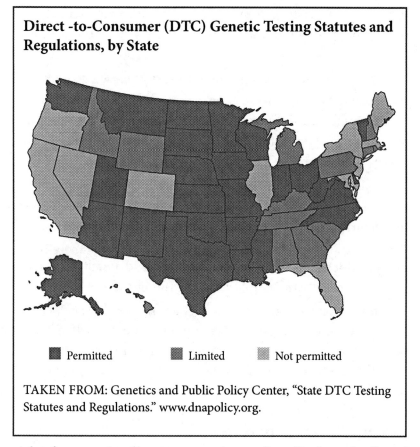

Direct -to-Consumer (DTC) Genetic Testing Statutes and Regulations, by State

Permitted   Limited   Not permitted

TAKEN FROM: Genetics and Public Policy Center, "State DTC Testing Statutes and Regulations." www.dnapolicy.org.

risks for certain diseases constitutes "medical testing" and whether the tests should be ordered only by a doctor.

Some of the less reputable companies make promises that go way beyond present capabilities. If they offer personalized advice about diet, lifestyle, and supplements based on DNA profiles, it's probably a scam to sell supplements. There is no scientific evidence to support those practices.

Questions About Pharmacogenetics

Pharmacogenetics promises to individualize prescriptions based on genetics, and it has already had some successes. A young patient with acute lymphocytic leukemia (ALL) might have died from her treatment if she'd been given the standard dose. Genetic testing showed she was unusually sensitive to 6-MP and her doctors knew to give her 1/5 of the standard dose.

The label for Abacavir (an HIV drug) now recommends that patients be tested for a gene that causes severe hypersensitivity reactions. Detecting genes associated with rare drug reactions can be very difficult, requiring studies with huge numbers for subjects.

A clinical trial of a new cancer drug Iressa showed little effect overall, and the FDA withdrew approval, but genetic testing determined that it worked very well for the 10% of patients who had a specific mutation. The current drug approval process doesn't take into account that a drug that fails for 90% of cancer patients might be lifesaving for 10%.

Some pharmacogenetic findings are not really very helpful. One gene raises the risk of developing myopathy when taking statin drugs, but that complication is uncommon, most cases are mild, and many patients with the incriminating genotype don't have the complication.

Promising Developments

The greatest promise of genome analysis is not in personal testing, but in research. Genetic analysis is redefining our concepts of illness. Psychiatric diagnoses have been based on subjective evaluations; genomics may make molecular classifications possible and totally change the approach to mental illness. Cancers that were lumped together are being found to differ significantly at the DNA level. A single gene has been linked to multiple diseases as different as diabetes, rheumatoid arthritis, and Crohn's disease.

In addition to our genome, we have a microbiome: the genes of the microbes that live on us and in us and greatly outnumber our own cells. These microbes contribute to illness, for instance the H. pylori bacteria that cause ulcers. We haven't even scratched the surface of what we may someday learn from sequencing the genes of our passengers.

Can bad genes be repaired? Experimental gene therapy is already being tested, but it won't be easy. Getting the gene to its desired location can be difficult, and then you have to get it to function in that new location and make sure it doesn't have adverse consequences (in some early trials, patients developed leukemia). But the potential is exciting: in one recent trial, color-blind monkeys were given color vision.

People with the CCR5Δ32 mutation are unusually resistant to HIV infection. An AIDS patient in Germany who developed leukemia was given a stem cell transplant to treat the leukemia. They deliberately chose a donor with the favorable mutation, and the recipient no longer has any signs of HIV infection.

Who Should Be Tested?

There are legal and social considerations. Genomic information might be used to deny employment or insurance. If a hereditary disease is identified, must other family members be notified? What if they would rather not know? If children are tested, should information be withheld until the child is old enough to give informed consent? Will people reject a potential marriage partner or choose adoption to avoid the risk of a hereditary disease? Testing can lead to rude surprises. Collins' book tells of an African American man who wanted to learn what part of Africa his ancestors came from. His DNA showed that he was 57% Indo-European, 39% Native American, 4% East Asian and 0% African!

Doctors order specific genetic tests for valid medical reasons. But direct-to-consumer testing is less justified. Should you get your DNA tested? Maybe, maybe not. You might learn some interesting-to-know facts, but it probably won't have any real impact on your health. We're not there yet. We've embarked on the journey but we're nowhere near as close to useful results as the tests' marketers would like us to believe.

> *"Of women whose ultrasounds showed a possible structural defect but whose fetuses were called normal by the visual chromosome exam, gene testing found problems in 6 percent."*

Prenatal Genetic Testing Helps Pregnant Women Detect Birth Defects

Marilynn Marchione

Prenatal genetic testing reveals more about potential health risks for high-risk pregnant women than conventional tests asserts Marilynn Marchione in the following viewpoint. A recent study revealed that genetic tests identified potential gene abnormalities in 6 percent of fetuses declared normal by ultrasound or amniocentesis, a risky testing procedure. Researchers claim that the goal of genetic testing is not to encourage women to abort pregnancies but to give them more information about causes, prognosis, and care. Although the tests are not always predictive, many women were glad to know what to look for and expect, she claims. Marchione is an award-winning medical writer for the Associated Press.

As you read, consider the following questions:

1. How does the cost of gene chip scanning differ from a visual exam?

2. What types of women were tested in the gene testing study?

3. According to University of Pennsylvania's Dr. Lorraine Dugoff, why might some couples not be happy that they ordered a genetic test?

A new study sets the stage for wider use of gene testing in early pregnancy. Scanning the genes of a fetus reveals far more about potential health risks than current prenatal testing does, say researchers who compared both methods in thousands of pregnancies nationwide.

More Revealing Results with Gene Testing

A surprisingly high number—6 percent—of certain fetuses declared normal by conventional testing were found to have genetic abnormalities by gene scans, the study found. The gene flaws can cause anything from minor defects such as a club foot to more serious ones such as mental retardation, heart problems and fatal diseases.

"This isn't done just so people can terminate pregnancies," because many choose to continue them even if a problem is found, said Dr. Ronald Wapner, reproductive genetics chief at Columbia University Medical Center in New York. "We're better able to give lots and lots of women more information about what's causing the problem and what the prognosis is and what special care their child might need."

He led the federally funded study, published in Thursday's [December 6, 2012] *New England Journal of Medicine.*

A second study in the journal found that gene testing could reveal the cause of most stillbirths, many of which remain a mystery now. That gives key information to couples agonizing over whether to try again.

The prenatal study of 4,400 women has long been awaited in the field, and could make gene testing a standard of care in cases where initial screening with an ultrasound exam suggests a structural defect in how the baby is developing, said Dr. Susan Klugman, director of reproductive genetics at New York's Montefiore Medical Center, which enrolled 300 women into the study.

"We can never guarantee the perfect baby but if they want everything done, this is a test that can tell a lot more," she said.

Many pregnant women are offered screening with an ultrasound exam or a blood test that can flag some common abnormalities such as Down syndrome, but these are not conclusive.

The next step is diagnostic testing on cells from the fetus obtained through amniocentesis, which is like a needle biopsy through the belly, or chorionic villus sampling, which snips a bit of the placenta. Doctors look at the sample under a microscope for breaks or extra copies of chromosomes that cause a dozen or so abnormalities.

The new study compared this eyeball method to scanning with gene chips that can spot hundreds of abnormalities and far smaller defects than what can be seen with a microscope. This costs $1,200 to $1,800 versus $600 to $1,000 for the visual exam.

Studying High-Risk Moms

In the study, both methods were used on fetal samples from 4,400 women around the country. Half of the moms were at higher risk because they were over 35. One-fifth had screening tests suggesting Down syndrome. One-fourth had ultrasounds suggesting structural abnormalities. Others sought screening for other reasons.

Three Types of Prenatal Genetic Testing

Amniocentesis

How It's Done: A long needle inserted through the mother's belly at 16 to 18 weeks slurps up some of the fluid surrounding the baby. . . .

What It Looks For: Chromosomal abnormalities like Down syndrome, genetic disorders like cystic fibrosis, neural tube defects like spina bifida.

Risks: Miscarriage, infection, Rh sensitization. . . .

Ultrasound

How It's Done: Sound waves passed through the uterus bounce off the fetus, producing an image. . . .

What It Looks For: A range of problems. Particularly, at the end of the first trimester, technicians measure the thickness of the back of the fetus's neck to identify signs of chromosomal defects. In the second half of pregnancy, ultrasound can check the baby's position, amount of amniotic fluid, and the condition of the placenta.

Risks: None. . . .

Cell-Free Fetal DNA Test

How It's Done: A blood draw at 10 weeks. . . .

What It Looks For: Down, Patau, and Edwards syndromes, sex-chromosome disorders like Turner and Klinefelter syndromes.

Risks: None.

Erin Biba, Wired, *December 24, 2012.*

"Some did it for anxiety—they just wanted more information about their child," Wapner said.

Of women whose ultrasounds showed a possible structural defect but whose fetuses were called normal by the visual chromosome exam, gene testing found problems in 6 percent—one out of 17.

"That's a lot. That's huge," Klugman said.

Gene tests also found abnormalities in nearly 2 percent of cases where the mom was older or ultrasounds suggested a problem other than a structural defect.

Dr. Lorraine Dugoff, a University of Pennsylvania high-risk pregnancy specialist, wrote in an editorial in the journal that gene testing should become the standard of care when a structural problem is suggested by ultrasound. But its value may be incremental in other cases and offset by the 1.5 percent of cases where a gene abnormality of unknown significance is found.

In those cases, "a lot of couples might not be happy that they ordered that test" because it can't give a clear answer, she said.

Ana Zeletz, a former pediatric nurse from Hoboken, N.J., had one of those results during the study. An ultrasound suggested possible Down syndrome; gene testing ruled that out but showed an abnormality that could indicate kidney problems—or nothing.

"They give you this list of all the things that could possibly be wrong," Zeletz said. Her daughter, Jillian, now 2, had some urinary and kidney abnormalities that seem to have resolved, and has low muscle tone that caused her to start walking later than usual.

"I am very glad about it," she said of the testing, because she knows to watch her daughter for possible complications like gout. Without the testing, "we wouldn't know anything, we wouldn't know to watch for things that might come up," she said.

The other study involved 532 stillbirths—deaths of a fetus in the womb before delivery. Gene testing revealed the cause in 87 percent of cases versus 70 percent of cases analyzed by the visual chromosome inspection method. It also gave more information on specific genetic abnormalities that couples could use to estimate the odds that future pregnancies would bring those risks.

The study was led by Dr. Uma Reddy of the National Institute of Child Health and Human Development.

> *"Before I had my son Gunner ... I didn't see prenatal diagnosis for what it really is, a tool to advance the eugenic agenda."*

Prenatal Genetic Testing Promotes Abortion

Kristan Hawkins

Prenatal genetic testing is not a tool to help prepare parents for children who suffer from diseases such as Down syndrome or cystic fibrosis, argues Kristan Hawkins in the following viewpoint. These tests are, in fact, tools to eliminate children that some believe are too costly for society, she claims. Unfortunately, Hawkins asserts, the government is involved in promoting this agenda, as it supports organizations that promote aborting children who suffer from Down syndrome and cystic fibrosis. People need to recognize the link between prenatal testing and abortion and promote a health care system that values all human life, even those with genetic diseases, she reasons. Hawkins leads Students for Life of America, a pro-life organization.

139

As you read, consider the following questions:

1. According to Hank Greely of Stanford's Center for Law and the Biosciences, how will the number of prenatal tests performed grow?

2. What did Hawkins say she had to accept when her son Gunner was diagnosed with cystic fibrosis?

3. According to Hawkins, what percentage of children with Down syndrome and cystic fibrosis were aborted?

In a January [2011] *Nature Magazine* article the head of Stanford's Center for Law and Biosciences, Hank Greely, said that within five years, genetic testing kits will be available over the counter that will predict not only whether a preborn baby has Down Syndrome, Cystic Fibrosis, or Tay Sachs disease, but also the baby's sex and eye color.

This is an alarming statement—one that, at first, many may not give a second thought [to], even some pro-lifers.

The Eugenic Agenda

In the same article, Greely estimates that the number of genetic tests performed on preborn babies will jump from the current 100,000 to over 3 million and that abortions will be viewed as a way to save money from being spent on "high cost children." Because who really wants "to bring a child into the world who will suffer and cause their family undue burden and emotional and financial hardship?"

Before I had my son Gunner, I knew that prenatal diagnosis was being used to eliminate children with Down Syndrome, but I didn't connect prenatal testing as the determining factor for abortions. My thinking was, "Well, it's good to have prenatal diagnosis for those parents who want to know and be prepared for the birth of their child." As a pro-life advocate, I obviously was and still am against abortion for any reason and believe that all persons have the right to exist, but

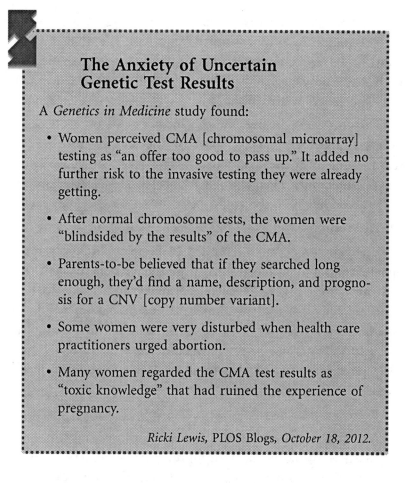

The Anxiety of Uncertain Genetic Test Results

A *Genetics in Medicine* study found:

- Women perceived CMA [chromosomal microarray] testing as "an offer too good to pass up." It added no further risk to the invasive testing they were already getting.

- After normal chromosome tests, the women were "blindsided by the results" of the CMA.

- Parents-to-be believed that if they searched long enough, they'd find a name, description, and prognosis for a CNV [copy number variant].

- Some women were very disturbed when health care practitioners urged abortion.

- Many women regarded the CMA test results as "toxic knowledge" that had ruined the experience of pregnancy.

Ricki Lewis, PLOS Blogs, October 18, 2012.

I didn't see prenatal diagnosis for what it really is, a tool to advance the eugenic agenda, I just thought of it as a modern medicine tool that can help prepare parents.

Looking beyond the fact that some prenatal diagnosis procedures can be deadly for the preborn child and that it is not always accurate, I now have deep convictions against the use of prenatal diagnosis.

Refusing Prenatal Genetic Tests

When my oldest son, Gunner, was diagnosed at 2 months with Cystic Fibrosis (CF), my faith and my world was turned upside down like any parent's would be.

I have had to learn to accept a lot of things—the fact that my precious baby boy will not have an easy life, that my husband and I will always struggle financially to provide him with everything he needs, and that his life may be dramatically shortened at any moment.

Not long ago during one of Gunner's doctor visits, a genetics counselor, who is a part of the Cystic Fibrosis care team, came into the exam room and asked how she could "help" our family. Even though I knew what she was going to say, I asked her how she could help.

Her response?

The genetics counselor replied that she could help arrange genetic testing for mine and my husband's sisters to see if they too carry the CF gene before they marry and decide to have children. She also told my husband and I that we would be "prime" candidates for in-vitro fertilization, which would allow us to create and select only embryos which do not have the Cystic Fibrosis for implantation, if we were considering having more children.

I refused her "help."

And last year, when I was pregnant with my 2nd son, Bear, I refused multiple requests for prenatal testing. And within minutes after his birth, I had to refuse multiple offers to insert an IUD into me, which would prevent the "risk" of having another child with Cystic Fibrosis.

You see, I refuse to accept the mentality that Gunner was a mistake and that if only I had gotten those prenatal tests, which I didn't undergo because of the risk to him, that he would not be on this earth today.

Promoting Prenatal Genetic Testing

A few months ago, I read two excellent articles by Mary Meehan in the *Human Life Review* about the history of prenatal diagnosis and our government's involvement in the promotion of the testing. Here are some of the highlights of those articles and other articles I have read in the past 2 years on this issue:

1. Eugenics is founded out of Darwinism, the notion that only the "fit" should survive and that certain types of people should not "use up" society's resources because they will not be adding to them.

2. In the mid-20th century, the American Eugenics Society realized that its name came with a negative connotation and changed its name to the American Genetics Society. Same people, same leaders, same ideas—just a different marketing scheme.

3. The March of Dimes has been a prime supporter of genetics and actually published a journal called *Birth Defects* until the mid-1990s. Their agenda is working—they are "curing" diseases in children by killing them in the womb—90% of Down Syndrome and CF children are aborted. (It is no wonder why they support Planned Parenthood.)

4. Planned Parenthood, the Goliath of the abortion business, is directly tied into the Eugenics/Genetics movement. We know this because of Margaret Sanger's writings and interviews about her own eugenics belief and quest to promote birth control to the poor and weak. Alan Guttmacher, Planned Parenthood's first president was also the Vice President of the American Eugenics Society, and the list of connections goes on between Planned Parenthood and Eugenics/Genetics. Watch the documentary *Maafa 21* for more information about this twisted connection.

5. Shockingly, eugenics is alive and well in America. I hear eugenic statements all the time even from people who do not realize they are doing it. Just last week, a You-

Tube video surfaced of Bill Gates, founder of Microsoft, talking to an audience [February 12, 2010, at the TED2010 Conference, Long Beach, CA] about how to reduce global CO_2 emissions. He gives an equation for how this can be accomplished—the first step reducing people. He thinks we can reduce the world's population by 10–15%, about 1 billion people, in the coming years through vaccines and reproductive "medicines".

(A side question to Mr. Gates—what vaccines are you referring to that will reduce the world's population? I want to stay away from those types!)

Today, we must begin the discussion about the link between prenatal testing, eugenics, abortion. And we must work to put into place a health care system in America that values all human life regardless of their genetic makeup.

"Providing [prenatal genetic testing] information might create what feels like a turning point . . . that could gradually shift what is normal."

Prenatal Genetic Testing Raises Serious Social Concerns

Carolyn Y. Johnson

In the following viewpoint, Carolyn Y. Johnson asserts that because prenatal genetic tests may lead some parents to terminate a pregnancy, these tests create ethical dilemmas for the medical community. Although the tests today are recommended only for high-risk pregnancies, their use may expand, reshaping the conditions under which parents decide whether to continue a pregnancy, she claims. Without information, making an educated choice may be difficult for those who do not know that while life with a child with Down syndrome is challenging, it also has its joys. As testing is expanded, she maintains, what people consider a normal child may change. Johnson is a science writer for the Boston Globe.

As you read, consider the following questions:

1. According to Johnson, why did expectant parents Trafford and Courtney Kane not feel good about their participation in a prenatal genetic testing study?

2. What did an *American Journal of Medical Genetics* study find about people with Down syndrome and their families?

3. In Johnson's opinion, what has driven the push for prenatal blood tests?

On a stormy Valentine's Day in 2007, Courtney Kane felt herself detach from her body and float up to the ceiling. She watched as the figure below, 19 weeks pregnant, reclined on a bed in an exam room, talking to a doctor and a genetic counselor.

A Mother's Story

Her husband, Trafford, was holding her hand. Her mother had come along for support. She felt as if the rest of the world had dropped away and they were alone, like characters frozen in a spotlight on a stage.

A detailed ultrasound had given the medical team a strong indication that the Kanes' baby had Down syndrome, and Courtney now found herself agreeing to have a long, thin needle inserted into her abdomen to retrieve amniotic fluid for genetic testing. The invasive test was uncomfortable and scary, and it carried a small risk of miscarriage.

The results wouldn't be known for a few days, so the family traveled back to their 200-year-old home in Swansea [Massachusetts], numb. The roof had started leaking and water was pooling on the dining room table, but they barely noticed.

When the Kanes were later asked to participate in a study that would help in the development of an alternative prenatal test that required only a tube of blood, they didn't hesitate. Courtney wanted to help other women avoid the invasive procedure, called amniocentesis.

Fast-forward to 2013.

In the short span of a year and a half, four companies in the United States have launched prenatal tests that use maternal blood to detect syndromes such as Down, which are caused by abnormal numbers of chromosomes, as early as nine or 10 weeks into pregnancy. Not all the companies have disclosed their sales, but tens of thousands of tests have been sold, and the underlying technology has the potential to reveal more. Last year, researchers demonstrated that a mother's blood could be used to reconstruct the entire genome of a fetus.

Meanwhile, rather than feel good about their contribution to this medical advance, the Kanes utterly regret the small role they played in helping push the technology forward. If the tests get more accurate and expand in use, as they seem poised to do, Courtney, 34, and Trafford, 32, expect that more families will opt for a seemingly harmless test very early in the pregnancy. Information, after all, is empowering. But information is also powerful in ways families don't always anticipate; a positive result can push them toward a crossroads, a decision point. The Kanes worry that fewer families will know the joys of Julia.

Insights and Dilemmas

The genome era—made possible by the ever-cheaper, ever-faster ability to read the DNA "book of life"—has brought ethical dilemmas along with biomedical insight. The medical community wrestles with questions about how genetic tests should be used and what information should be disclosed to patients.

But in perhaps no other area are the questions raised by the evolving technology as morally fraught as when they in-

© 2005 Antonio Nerilicon, El Economista, Mexico. www.politicalcartoons.com/Cagle Cartoons Inc.

volve a 10-week-old fetus, when parents may use the test re-sults to decide whether to terminate or continue a pregnancy.

Today, use of the new prenatal blood tests is limited. Medi-cal groups recommend them only for high-risk pregnancies, including women 35 and older. They currently screen for a small number of chromosomal syndromes. A positive result must be followed up by more invasive tests for a definitive diagnosis. Many, however, anticipate the eventual expansion of the tests—both to a larger swath of pregnant women and to a wider catalog of genetic conditions and disorders.

Vastly increasing the number of women who learn about the genetic traits of their baby early on has the potential to re-shape the medical and social experience of pregnancy, in the way it has already altered the lives of families that learn they are having a child with Down syndrome.

Advocates for the Down syndrome community worry that wider prenatal testing will mean more expectant parents re-ceive an alarming test result without sufficient information to make an informed choice about whether to terminate or con-tinue the pregnancy.

"I think Down syndrome is genetics' canary in a coal mine," said Dr. Brian Skotko, a physician at Massachusetts General Hospital who co-leads a clinic focused on caring for people with Down.

"There are today 250,000 Americans with Down syndrome, only [about] 50,000 away from being reclassified as a rare dis-ease," Skotko said. "We are, in the moment, potentially seeing through our society's choices the elimination of a people."

Recalibrating Perceptions

Skotko has a younger sister, Kristin, with Down, and he has performed surveys that have helped recalibrate perceptions of the lives of individuals with Down. In studies published in the *American Journal of Medical Genetics*, he found that 99 per-cent of people with Down report being happy with their lives, and 79 percent of parents credited having a child with Down with giving them a more positive outlook.

But he also was a reviewer for a brochure that mentions abortion as one of the options expectant parents can consider, and he describes himself as pro-information when it comes to genetic testing.

Women who knew their baby's diagnosis ahead of time had more positive feelings about their pregnancy and their birth experiences than those who found out when their child was born.

Are the new, noninvasive prenatal tests "something to worry about or something to celebrate? The answer is yes," said Hank Greely, a bioethicist at Stanford Law School. "It depends on who you are and what you believe."

Legitimate Concerns

He said that a safe test that allows women to get accurate information about their pregnancy—including the challenges they may face—is a benefit. But the concerns of people within the Down syndrome community are real, because a shrinking community of people with Down could lead to less support for research and treatment, and reduce societal acceptance of people with the condition.

"Those are really legitimate concerns for the Down community and I think they should be legitimate concerns for all of us," Greely said. "Disabilities, disadvantage, heartbreak, tragedy sometimes bring out the best in people. But we still, in general, set up our society to try to avoid them."

Before the advent of the new technology, only 2 percent of pregnant women opted for the invasive genetic tests. The new tests, however, are far simpler—perhaps one of a handful of blood draws that a pregnant woman would get during a routine visit. Women are supposed to receive counseling before agreeing to the test, but more women may opt to take an essentially harmless blood test, perhaps without fully thinking through the types of results they may receive. If the tests do expand to other conditions, that means that an increasing amount of information, which typically came after a baby was born, may be divined ahead of time.

"I think this really challenges couples to answer two essential questions," Skotko said. "Their own personal questions on when does life begin for them, and what forms of human conditions are considered valuable."

Learning About Down Syndrome

It was two days after the amniocentesis when Courtney Kane got the news over the phone: Her first baby had Down syndrome. She fell to the floor sobbing and curled up in a ball. She called her mother, a teacher, who left school early to be there.

That day, the Kanes went back for a meeting with the genetic counselor, who told them they had three options: to continue the pregnancy, terminate it, or put the baby up for adoption. Courtney and Trafford did not know any people with Down syndrome; it wasn't a risk they had been focused on, since they were both young and healthy.

They asked what other people did in their situation. The counselor told them the vast majority, 90 percent of people, terminated the pregnancies.

"We were pretty overwhelmed with the high statistics," Courtney said. "We thought, there must be a reason why."

They left the appointment with two books. One was a parents' guide to Down syndrome. It described the condition, caused by an extra chromosome, explaining that it causes children to experience delays in physical and mental development of varying severity. The other was a collection of stories from women who had chosen to terminate their pregnancies for a variety of reasons.

Overwhelmed by Options

The Kanes started the weekend overwhelmed by the options. If they chose to continue the pregnancy, their baby would need open-heart surgery in addition to having Down syndrome.

They felt they didn't know enough. All the information made it hard to answer the one question they cared most about: Would their child be able to have a good quality of life? Would he or she be happy? They begged close family members for advice. It would have been easier if they had strong religious views and opposed abortion, but the Kanes do not. For one tormented day, they seriously contemplated ending the pregnancy, trying to understand what that would mean.

"We spent a day inside of that feeling," Trafford recalled.

Courtney had a nightmare that night. Her mother had stayed over and Courtney crawled into bed with her the next morning. Connie Ward wanted the couple to come to their own decision.

"I remember reading, restating facts . . . asking questions with as little judgment," Ward said. "I knew how Courtney felt; I just know her."

Almost intuitively, without a big debate or talk that either can remember, Courtney and Trafford realized they had both reached a decision as they milled around the kitchen Sunday morning. It was sunny outside. There was no question. They would have this baby.

The Upside of Prenatal Blood Tests

The push for prenatal blood tests is driven by simple reasoning: to reduce the number of invasive procedures that cause fear in the mother and a small risk to the baby while also providing information about genetic conditions to help guide the pregnancy.

Last December, the American College of Obstetricians and Gynecologists and the Society for Maternal-Fetal Medicine released a committee opinion calling the new prenatal blood tests a technology with "tremendous potential as a screening tool" for abnormal numbers of chromosomes. The tests will allow many women with high-risk pregnancies to forgo the riskier tests, according to Dr. Diana Bianchi, executive director of the Mother Infant Research Institute at Tufts Medical Center.

Several companies are now conducting clinical trials to determine whether their screening tests could be used in the general population of pregnant women. They hope to demonstrate that the tests are more accurate than conventional screening used in women not at high risk. Conventional screening has a false positive rate of about 5 percent and also may indicate there is a low risk of a problem when a fetus does have a chromosomal syndrome.

Bianchi sees a further upside to the new tests, which can provide earlier diagnosis. The benefit, she says, is not just that women could make decisions about whether to continue pregnancies based on information about the fetus, but that the growing area of fetal medicine might have more time to intervene.

"You could conceivably have 30 weeks to treat a condition," said Bianchi, who last week presented early data at the meeting of the Society for Gynecologic Investigation in Florida showing the effects of an antioxidant drug in mice with a form of Down syndrome. The drug was administered through the pregnant mother's food and was continued until the offspring were 8 to 10 weeks old. Mice that received the treatment were less hyperactive and displayed more normal exploratory behavior. Bianchi's hypothesis is that the drug may reduce oxidative stress that interferes with normal brain development.

But Dov Fox, a fellow at Georgetown University Law Center, said that the tests may lead to a subtle societal shift that often gets left out of the debate. Providing the information might create what feels like a turning point for many—compelling a decision to do something or not do something that could gradually shift what is normal.

"It also exerts social pressure on parents to terminate pregnancy for fear of criticism or reproach from people who regard the choice—their child with a disability—as negligent, or irresponsible," Fox said. "This increasing willingness to prevent the birth of children with impairments or genetic abnormalities may, moreover, bring a tendency to exclude rather than accommodate people whose abilities fail to meet the demands" of the everyday world.

The Joys of Julia

A test returns results in black and white terms—positive or negative, or a risk expressed as a set of numbers. It can't convey what a whole life would feel like.

In July 2007, when Julia was born, her mother instantly recognized the physical features of Down; she had been reading about them for months. Julia had slightly upturned eyes. Trafford recalls she had low muscle tone—she was a little bit floppy.

But as Courtney looked down at the baby in her arms, she felt that all the books she'd read had given her only the vaguest hints of how her daughter's life would unfold. The way she and Trafford would hold their breath through her open-heart surgery. The way they would worry about Julia as they tried to get her to gain an ounce. The way they would get to know their head-strong, social little girl who wiggles her feet when she is excited and clinks her red popsicle with everyone's cup in a joyous toast after dinner. The way she would have to be painstakingly taught how to jump and walk and practically everything else—and how that struggle would make it all that much sweeter.

Now, the parents have watched as her younger brother, Oliver, 2, seemed to learn faster from Julia—and is now helping to accelerate her development. As he has learned to string words together into sentences, Julia makes more of an effort, too.

The Kanes say they are part of a club that no one would think they want to join, but that they would never want to leave.

There is something else Courtney vividly remembers from the first time she held her daughter.

In some ways, it is an emotion specific to having a child she knew would be slow to speak, might never get married, and might never live independently. But in other ways, it's the same feeling all parents have.

As she gazed into her daughter's blue eyes, Courtney heard a voice in her head say, "Please, just love me. I'm not what you expected, but please just love me. . . . I need you guys to be on my team."

Periodical and Internet Sources Bibliography

The following articles have been selected to supplement the diverse views presented in this chapter.

Robert Alison	"Genetic Screening Moral Minefield," *Winnipeg (Manitoba) Free Press*, June 24, 2013.
Ken Alltucker	"Genetic Tests Start to Inflate Nation's Health-Care Bill," *Arizona Republic*, March 18, 2012.
Sharon Begley	"Back to the Genetic Future: Why Family Medical History Is Key," *Newsweek*, November 22, 2010.
Erin Biba	"This Simple Blood Test Reveals Birth Defects—And the Future of Pregnancy," *Wired*, December 24, 2012.
Eryn Brown	"Not Every Woman Should Get the BRCA Gene Test, US Task Force Says," *Los Angeles Times*, April 1, 2013.
Hastings Center	"Personalized Medicine: Will It Work? Where Will It Take Us?" *Hastings Center Report*, vol. 40 no. 5, September/October 2010.
Angelina Jolie	"My Medical Choice," *New York Times*, May 13, 2013.
Karen Kaplan	"Simple Prenatal Genetic Tests May Lead to Healthier Babies—And More Abortions," *Los Angeles Times*, January 20, 2011.
Gregory M. Lamb	"How Reliable Is Personal DNA Testing?" *Christian Science Monitor*, September 15, 2010.
Ricki Lewis	"Prenatal Genetic Testing: When Is It 'Toxic Knowledge'?" *DNA Science Blog*, October 18, 2012.
Alexandra Roginski	"Unnatural Selection," *Chronicle of Higher Education*, June 21, 2013.

OPPOSING VIEWPOINTS® SERIES

CHAPTER 4

What Is the Impact of Collecting Human Genetic Information?

Chapter Preface

Policy makers have long been challenged by how best to balance the need to solve crime while protecting civil liberties and rights. For many years, law enforcement has used DNA collected from criminals to identify them as suspects in past and future crimes. However, using their DNA to catch family members who commit crimes is relatively new and one of several controversies in the debate over the collection of human genetic information. One of the early examples of the potential of familial DNA searches was its use to arrest a possible serial killer in California. Over a twenty-year period, as many as ten women were murdered in the Los Angeles area. The police dubbed the killer the Grim Sleeper as he appeared to go dormant between murders committed in the late 1980s and those starting in 2002. During that time, police had collected saliva left on the bodies of these murdered women, but received no hits from the FBI's Combined DNA Index System (CODIS) and had no other useful leads. However, in 2008, California adopted a familial DNA search policy, and the police decided to test the salvia using a familial DNA search. They identified Christopher Franklin as a familial match. Christopher had provided his DNA upon conviction for a felony weapons charge. Once his father, Lonnie David Franklin, was identified as a suspect, undercover officers obtained a pizza crust discarded by the suspect that matched the DNA left on the murder victims' bodies. He was arrested in 2010 but as of December 2013 had yet to be tried. While some cite cold cases such as the murders committed by the Grim Sleeper as evidence of the benefits of familial DNA searches, others raise civil liberties and civil rights concerns.

Opponents argue that while criminals may have no expectation of privacy, family members of those convicted of crimes do have such an expectation. Thus, argues American Civil

Liberties Union senior staff counsel Adam Schwartz, familial DNA database searches unconstitutionally expand the scope of such searches. "The result is a massive expansion of the effective reach of forensic DNA databases: from the 9 million people now in the FBI's DNA database, to the tens of millions of additional people who are their parents, siblings, and children."[1] Moreover, Schwartz asserts, familial DNA databases create a special class of people subject to a greater burden: those related to convicted felons and thus who may be come suspects due to familial DNA testing. Then, there were those not related to criminals and thus will not become suspects. "Being subject to a criminal investigation is burdensome. Police might question friends, neighbors, and coworkers. The cloud of criminal suspicion can disrupt work and family relationships."[2] Of even greater concern to many people is the disparate impact familial DNA searches will have on African Americans. One study concluded that 17 percent of the African American population is related to a person in the DNA database compared to only 4 percent of Caucasian Americans. New York University law professor and familial DNA opponent Erin Murphy asserts, "The thing that I find troubling is that we're saying that certain people who haven't done anything but are related to people who have also forfeit their genetic privacy."[3]

In answer to familial DNA database critics, advocates of California's policy argue that familial searches are used only as a last resort and only to generate leads in very serious crimes. In response to the claim that these searches violate privacy, Los Angeles County district attorney Jackie Lacey responds, "We think having the certainty outweighs the potential pri-

1. Adam Schwartz, *DNA Familial Testing: Civil Liberties and Civil Rights Concerns*, Symposium on Familial DNA Searching, Center on Wrongful Convictions, Northwestern University School of Law, March 3, 2011.
2. *Ibid.*
3. Quoted in Eryn Brown, "Study Probes DNA Search Method That Led to 'Grim Sleeper' Suspect," *Los Angeles Times*, August 15, 2013.

vacy issues."[4] Others claim that familial DNA searches are far more useful and precise than traffic stops or stop-and-frisk searches, particularly since they are used only to generate leads. According to Frederick Bieber, an authority on familial DNA searches and a medical geneticist at Brigham and Women's Hospital in Boston, "There's no conflict between developing an investigative lead and protecting the privacy and dignity of individuals."[5]

Whether familial DNA databases effectively balance the competing interests of solving crime and protecting liberties remains subject to vigorous debate. The authors in the following chapter present their views in other controversies surrounding the question of the impact of collecting human genetic information. Although the familial DNA database debate continues, few states have established policies regarding familial DNA and how it should be used. Whether the use of this genetic information will expand remains to be seen.

4. *Ibid.*
5. *Ibid.*

> *"Chief among the downsides [of human genetics research] are increased numbers of widely-available databases . . . as well as increasing incidences of loss of privacy and discrimination."*

The Collection of Human Genetic Information Poses Threats to Civil Liberties

Philip L. Bereano

Governments and private organizations are collecting an enormous amount of genetic information asserts Philip L. Bereano in the following viewpoint. Although this information can be useful, the threat to civil liberties is significant, he claims. DNA databases threaten Fourth Amendment prohibitions against unreasonable searches and seizures. In addition, large genetic databases pose a threat to privacy, which can, in turn, lead to genetic discrimination. Furthermore, Bereano argues, genetic data allow elites to determine what traits are valuable, further increasing the gap between rich and poor. Bereano, cofounder of the Council for Responsible Genetics, is professor of technology and public policy at the University of Washington in Seattle.

Philip L. Bereano, "Genes and Civil Liberties," ActionBioscience.com, January 2013. Copyright © 2013 by ActionBioscience.com. All rights reserved. Reproduced by permission.

As you read, consider the following questions:

1. According to Bereano, what is the impact of reserving control of genetic technologies for elites?

2. What factors does the American Civil Liberties Union (ACLU) believe should be considered when collecting genetic information for a database?

3. In Berean's opinion, what has raised the public profile of the controversy over genetic enhancement?

"The power to assemble a permanent national DNA database of all offenders who have committed any of the crimes listed has catastrophic potential. If placed in the hands of an administration that chooses to 'exalt order at the cost of liberty' [such a] database could be used to repress dissent or, quite literally, to eliminate political opposition . . . Today, the court has opted for comprehensive DNA profiling of the least protected among us, and in so doing, has jeopardized us all." Judge Stephen R. Reinhardt, dissenting in *U.S. v. Kincade*, 9th Circuit Court of Appeals, 2004, a ruling that allowed parolees to be compelled to provide a DNA sample.

Genetic technologies provide a new arena for tensions between our cherished ideals of liberty, order, justice, and fairness. Newspapers report the wonders such genetic knowledge can bring, but less often the threats for which these "advances" are also responsible. In reality, the ability to identify people and determine elements of their genetic profiles has significant downsides.

The dominant ideology in Western society holds that the only problems caused by technologies are either unintended side effects or abuses. However, technologies are not designed to benefit all segments of society equally. Because of their size, scale, and requirements for capital investments and knowledge, modern technologies can allow already-powerful groups to consolidate their powers.

The Problem with Databases

Many government and private programs collect biological tissues, DNA samples, and the results of genetic analyses. At the same time, tests for new specific genes are being developed and DNA databases are being shared among individuals and organizations. Although these practices themselves raise policy issues, the uses of such information (computerized and easily correlated) also put civil liberties at risk. These efforts often reflect a belief that genes determine who a person is and what he or she is likely to do, and thus how society should treat the individual. Yet despite talk about genes for homosexuality, intelligence, or violence, such complex behaviors are likely the result of many biological and non-biological factors.

The use of the genetic technologies for control is reserved for elites—medical professionals, government functionaries, the very wealthy and their agents. And the people whose data is collected will often be those with little power. Thus employers test employees, insurance companies and health organizations test patients, college officials test students, and legislators pass bills proposing to test disempowered groups (e.g., prisoners).

The US Department of Defense (DoD) insists on taking DNA samples from all of its personnel, ostensibly to aid in the identification of those killed in action or military accidents, although its database has also been used for law enforcement purposes. Yet the samples are to be kept for 50 years (long after people have left active duty), the program includes civilian employees who are not in harm's way, the agency refuses to issue regulations barring all third-party use, and the Department will not accept waivers from the next of kin of subjects not wanting to donate tissues.

The American Civil Liberties Union (ACLU) suggests some factors to consider when data is being collected that will go into a systemic database:

- Personal information should not be collected without individuals' informed consent;

- Mandatory collection must be limited to what is required to achieve legitimate policy objectives. Exceptions should require statutory authority and information must be destroyed or made anonymous as soon as the authorized use is completed;

- The degree of control an individual has over such information should depend on how "sensitive" it is (e.g., its potential to cause the person harm if made accessible or misused and the importance the person places on its confidentiality);

- Information on ethnic origin, political or religious beliefs, health status, and sexual and financial life are often considered sensitive. Possible harms include limits to a person's economic, social, or political opportunities and needless embarrassment, stigma, or threats to the person's safety.

Forensic Use of Genetic Information

Every politician is in favor of solving crime, yet the Founding Fathers still saw the need for the Fourth Amendment to prohibit unreasonable searches and seizures, and the constitutions of many states have even stronger provisions protecting privacy. Since the 1990s the FBI has been promoting the genetic screening of criminals for use in criminal investigations, with results being used to establish state DNA identification databanks and compiled into a single national data library, the Combined DNA Index System (CODIS). Yet the data—from about 10 million Americans so far—include samples from individuals whose crimes have low recidivism rates and whose crimes don't usually leave tissue DNA behind. The US Attorney General has set up a program to "assess criminal justice system delays in the analysis of DNA evidence and develop recommendations to eliminate those delays" which began in March of 2003; however, there is little evidence of concern for the civil liberties aspects of the program. Access to CODIS is available to all law enforcement and judicial proceedings and, in a somewhat limited scope, to criminal defendants.

An increasingly common development is the collection and filing in CODIS of DNA from people who are merely accused and arrested, seemingly violating the Constitutional presumption of innocence. In 2012, the highest court in Maryland ruled that DNA collection from arrestees violated the Fourth Amendment; according to *The New York Times*, of the 10,666 samples collected in the state last year from arrestees, only 10 were from people who were later convicted. In other words, for 99.9% of these "searches" it is hard to argue there is a valid criminal justice function being served. The issue is also before the Supreme Court of Vermont. In the meantime, the US Supreme Court has put the Maryland ruling on hold, indicating a likely review during its 2012–13 term.

On the other hand, specific matching of DNA from crime-scene samples and from suspects or people convicted of crimes (as opposed to using a pre-existing databank) has resulted in the exoneration of many falsely convicted individuals. In about a quarter of these cases, the wrongly convicted defendants made confessions or gave incriminating statements, thus suggesting that existing investigative procedures often involve coercion or, at [the] very least, fail to protect the presumption of innocence. Interestingly, many prosecutors and judges resist this sort of post-trial testing despite the fact that testing has led to the apprehension of the actual perpetrator.

Another civil liberties concern is that racial disparities so evident in the criminal justice system are also reflected in the databanks, thereby perpetuating the problem. Additionally, some proponents argue that current DNA collection techniques involve "only a mouth swab," insisting this makes the procedure less "invasive" than taking blood samples and meeting the legal standard of reasonable searches.

Maintaining Genetic Privacy

Genetic privacy, like medical privacy in general, involves questions of the dignity and integrity of the individual. Are the genetic data accurate? Can individuals access their own files? Can the donor correct inaccurate data? Are the custodians faithful and are technical security systems protecting the data where possible? Does the individual have control over which third parties are allowed access, and under what conditions? Many of the factors noted in the ACLU Policy above are directed toward addressing such privacy concerns.

Federal law has increasingly given attention to medical records privacy, especially in light of the growing trend toward computerization of medical information. The Health Insurance Portability and Accountability Act (HIPAA), 1996, imposes significant federal rules about privacy for health information—including genetic data—held by health care providers, group insurance programs (including Medicaid, Medicare, and Veterans Affairs), and "health care clearinghouses" (mainly billing services). It does not cover employment, individually purchased health insurance, or life insurance, even if these records contain health information.

Under the HIPAA statute, the "Privacy Rule" was promulgated in 2002, requiring covered organizations to provide patients with a notice describing how it will protect health information, including the patient's right to see the records and make corrections, learn how it has been used, and request additional protections. A "Security Rule" covers administrative, physical, and technical safeguards that organizations use to assure the confidentiality, integrity, and availability of electronic protected health information. However, privacy issues continue to arise with regard to other collections of DNA, such as CODIS, collection by the DoD, etc.

Biobanks Hold Risks

Biobanks are being created for good reasons. Researchers are desperate to get more-more samples, more analyses, more health records, more data, from more people, with more diseases, in more different settings. And they are right to be eager. Massive quantities of data may allow us to tease out the causes of various diseases and give us leads toward prevention, treatment, or cures. . . .

But these biobanks also hold risks. The people whose tissue, DNA, or health records are stored in biobanks could be harmed. And cases of such harm could prompt a backlash, ultimately slowing medical progress.

Henry T. Greely, GeneWatch, *Feb.–Mar. 2011.*

The Threat of Genetic Discrimination

Scientists working with the Council for Responsible Genetics have documented hundreds of cases in which healthy people have been denied medical insurance or employment on the basis of genetic "predictions." Yet few genetic diseases follow inevitably from having a specific genetic variant; most are probabilistic in occurrence. Genetic tests—which have inherent limits—cannot tell us if a genetic mutation *will become manifest*; likewise, if it does so, tests cannot tell us *when* in life this will occur or *how severe* the condition will be. In addition, many genetic conditions can be controlled or treated by interventions and environmental changes, which is why governments have mandated for decades that newborns be tested for phenylketonuria (PKU) and treated if the condition is found.

This discrimination was partially addressed when the HIPAA was implemented, which prohibited commercial health insurers from excluding people because of past or present medical conditions, including predisposition to certain diseases. HIPAA specifically states that genetic information in the absence of a current diagnosis is not a pre-existing condition; however, it does not prevent covered health plans from requesting genetic information from individuals as a part of the insurance underwriting process.

After many attempts, specific federal legislation finally passed in 2008 (the Genetic Information Nondiscrimination Act, or "GINA") addressing genetic discrimination in health insurance and employment. The Departments of Labor, Health and Human Services, and the Treasury administer the use of genetic information in group and individual health insurance, and employment enforcement is under the Equal Employment Opportunity Commission (EEOC). GINA makes it illegal to discriminate on the basis of genetic information (including the genetic information of family members) and restricts entities such as employers, employment agencies, and labor organizations from seeking genetic information. The disclosure of genetic information to third parties is limited as well.

Starting in 2014, prohibitions against health insurance plans discriminating on the basis of health status are amplified under the Affordable Care Act. The act explicitly lists "genetic information" among the health status-related factors which cannot be used to establish rules for eligibility or coverage. However, sellers of life insurance, disability insurance, and long-term care insurance can still use genetic data to discriminate against applicants.

The Prospect of Eugenics Programs

The availability of genetic data may seem to justify the creation of new human beings that lack specific, undesirable genetic variants, which raises additional concerns both about loss of privacy and increased opportunities for discrimination by powerful entities. In such a world, the desire for perfectionism and the ability to predict a baby's characteristics would replace tolerance for natural variation and diversity. Powerful scientists have already called for programs of eugenics, cleverly labeled as "genetic enhancement," to create more appealing suites of characteristics in individuals. Articles and television shows on "designer babies" were commonplace as many as ten years ago and, in conjunction with the 2012 Olympics, stories on "super athletes" were carried in the media, all of which raised the public profile of this controversial topic.

It's one thing to be curious about "genetic foreknowledge," but when does that carry over into control of genetic futures—of children, for example? Genetic tests are conducted not only on prospective parents, but are now available to test fetuses for potential "genetic problems." The newly developed techniques in the field of synthetic biology could potentially provide additional powerful tools and make them more widely available for similar ends.

Could parental genetic decisions actually limit the civil liberties of children? There is a dystopian possibility—the creation of human-animal chimeras. After all, we have 98% genetic similarity to an ape (and 75% to a pumpkin for that matter!), suggesting that creation of chimeras is quite possible. Although the U.S. Patent Office has ruled that chimeras are ineligible for patenting, will they be considered sufficiently "human" to be accorded civil rights? . . .

Although human genetics research and development are usually presented as "advances," they may also be setting back our civil liberties on many fronts. Chief among the downsides are increased numbers of widely-available databases that correlate many facets of people's biology, lives, and activities, as well as increasing incidences of loss of privacy and discrimination. While federal legislation and administrative rules have begun to address these problems, private and governmental data mining grows rapidly as new technological formats are developed and a technological rationality (i.e., "more information is better") continues to hold sway over public opinion. As society becomes more familiar with genetics, privacy violations and discrimination may decrease but—at the same time—the rationales for increasing the numbers of public information/DNA databases also increases. These negative consequences need to be more fully considered in any public policy decisions about genetic technologies.

"Ordinary Americans are more likely to see benefits than dangers in genomic science—despite the fact that genomics is not well known."

Americans Are Optimistic About the Benefits of Genomic Information

Jennifer Hochschild, Alex Crabill, and Maya Sen

In the following viewpoint, Jennifer Hochschild, Alex Crabill, and Maya Sen argue that Americans are generally optimistic about genetic technology, even though the technology is complex. In their study, the authors found that Americans generally believe the benefits of genetic technology outweigh the risks. In fact, Americans believe that genetic testing should be widely available; they support government involvement in genomic science and are willing to contribute DNA samples for research. Despite the knowledge gap, Americans remain relatively confident in genomic science. Jennifer Hochschild is professor of government and African American studies at Harvard University; Alex Crabill conducts research for the Project on Genomics, Politics, and Policy at Harvard University; Maya Sen is political science professor at Rochester University.

Jennifer Hochschild, Alex Crabill, and Maya Sen, "Technology Optimism or Pessimism: How Trust in Science Shapes Policy Attitudes Toward Genomic Science," *Issues in Technology*, no. 21, December 2012. Copyright © 2012 by The Brookings Institution. All rights reserved. Reproduced by permission.

As you read, consider the following questions:

1. How do Hochschild, Crabill, and Sen explain how people assess and perceive risk?

2. What are some of the concerns expressed by genomic science pessimists, in the authors' view?

3. In the authors' opinion, what are some of the concerns even genomic science optimists have about elites who generate or oversee genomic science?

Just as physics gained public visibility and ideological contention as it matured over the twentieth century, so genomic science will gain public visibility and competing normative valences as it becomes increasingly important during the twenty-first century. The new biology can help to solve many of humankind's most serious problems, or it can reinforce racial hierarchy and enhance governmental surveillance. Genomic scientists will protect our lives and our planet—or scientists are tampering dangerously with nature.

As of 2013, the production and use of genomics has been lightly regulated; court cases addressing medical or individual uses of genomics are rare and politicians' engagement even rarer. The American public is just beginning to learn about genomic science, its likely uses, and its potential benefits and harms. This relative vacuum permits social scientists to explore how innovations in genomics research are moving into the public arena; rarely do scholars have the chance to watch a new policy regime emerge, especially in such an important and fraught field. As public opinion develops, it may help to shape government funding, regulation, and legislation. Most importantly, to the degree that biology becomes in this century what physics was in the last—a powerful, somewhat mysterious force influencing the destinies of individuals, countries, and the globe—it is essential for any democratic polity to examine what people know, want, believe, and fear about it.

Those views will surely change as the science changes, but baseline analyses will enable political actors to know where people are starting. . . .

We conclude, first, that public attitudes toward genomic science are coherent and intelligible, perhaps surprisingly so given how new and complex the substantive issues are, and, second, that citizens differ from most social scientists, legal scholars, and policy advocates in their overall embrace of genomics' possibilities for benefitting society.

Technology Optimism, Pessimism, and Perceptions of Risk

Intuitively, technology optimism or pessimism is a measure of a person's level of risk seeking or risk aversion. More formally, technology optimism is the "underestimation and neglect of uncertainty" in favor of "widely shared speculative promise." An optimist "is centered on advancement concerns. . . . [He or she is driven] by motivations for attaining growth and supports *eager strategies* of seeking possible gains even at the risk of committing errors or accepting some loss." Examples are not hard to find. The genomics researcher Mary Claire King describes her postdoctoral Fellows as "banging down the doors at 7 a.m. so they can get to work and see what happened [in the lab] overnight." Entrepreneurs pursue profit from drug development; doctors seek diagnoses and targeted treatments; patients seek cures; individuals seek roots and family ties; legal advocates seek punishment for the guilty and exoneration for the falsely convicted.

In contrast, technology pessimism is the overestimation of threat and harmful impact and insufficient attention to benefits or to people's ability to respond appropriately to risk. A pessimist "is centered on security concerns. . . [and] supports *vigilant strategies* of protecting against possible losses even at the risk of missing opportunities of potential gains." Here too examples abound. Genewatch UK warns that "an over-emphasis on genetic explanations and solutions to these problems [. . . as diverse as hunger, crime, climate change and cancer] can mean that underlying social, economic and environmental issues are ignored," and that "commitments to particular assumptions about science, technology, nature and society are often made behind closed doors, with insufficient public scrutiny." A deep technology pessimist anticipates that medical benefits will appear only in the distant future if at all, while genomic science risks reifying the concept of race, introducing new forms of discrimination through genetic inheritance, tempting people into the pursuit of designer babies, and introducing "Frankenfoods" and judicial genomic surveillance.

Technology optimism or pessimism is an element of the broader psychological phenomenon of "perception of risk." Most researchers on the subject agree that it stems from non-experts' [or experts'] difficulty in estimating danger precisely. People lack relevant information and analytic frameworks; they receive contradictory messages from media and opinion leaders; risks may be intrinsically uncertain or not known; psychological proclivities shape reception of messages. Risk assessment may have as much to do with a person's cultural or social context as with his or her cognitive balancing act or actual knowledge—that is, as much to do with the person as the object being assessed. . . .

Almost anything can affect perceptions of risk and roughly the same variables appear to generate excessive optimism as excessive pessimism. That rather mundane conclusion is not much help to political actors or policy makers; our goal is to show patterns of optimism/pessimism more clearly and to clarify their implications and explanations in one important arena.

Pessimism in Genomic Science

Predictions about genomic science are indeed sometimes deeply pessimistic and motivated by security concerns. Some

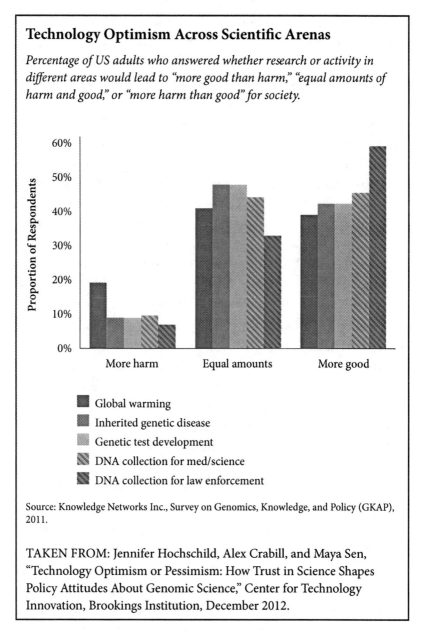

Technology Optimism Across Scientific Arenas

Percentage of US adults who answered whether research or activity in different areas would lead to "more good than harm," "equal amounts of harm and good," or "more harm than good" for society.

Source: Knowledge Networks Inc., Survey on Genomics, Knowledge, and Policy (GKAP), 2011.

TAKEN FROM: Jennifer Hochschild, Alex Crabill, and Maya Sen, "Technology Optimism or Pessimism: How Trust in Science Shapes Policy Attitudes About Genomic Science," Center for Technology Innovation, Brookings Institution, December 2012.

ethicists fear that in-vitro fertilization, combined with pre-implantation or prenatal genetic testing, is the first step toward genetic selection. At best, even if genetic selection were eventually deemed acceptable, which many oppose, it will exacerbate social inequalities by being available only to well-off parents. At worst, fetal genetic testing could rehabilitate eugenics through efforts to create ideal humans without disability, disfavored race, low intelligence, or other purported flaws.

Pessimists also worry that insurers and employers will use genetic information to deny coverage or jobs in order to avoid health care expenses associated with genetic predispositions to illness, obesity, or other conditions. The Genetic Information Non-Discrimination Act (GINA) of 2008 is intended to address these concerns by prohibiting health insurers and employers from engaging in genetic discrimination. But GINA excludes life, disability, or long-term care insurance and says nothing about settings beyond the workplace. Those "centered on security concerns" still have plenty to worry about.

Anxiety about American racial dynamics raises new issues: will researchers engage in "searches for a biological basis for criminal behavior"? Arguably only a small step separates the use of race as a shorthand for distinguishing phenotypes or the use of race as a shorthand for identifying populations with propensities to violence or sexual aggression. And the first race so identified, many anticipate, will be African Americans. Pessimists fear that "we are ill-prepared to respond to the complex challenges posed by racial arguments bobbing in the unstoppable tide of genetic research."

Forensic DNA databanks offer yet more fertile ground for technology pessimism. Due to disproportions in arrests, immigrant detentions, felony convictions, or simply family size, about 40 percent of the people with samples in the almost 10 million person federal forensic database (CODIS) are black. Hispanics are also disproportionately represented. By one plausible calculation, at least one fifth of the black population, compared with only one-twentieth of non-blacks, is under genetically based police surveillance either directly or through the technique of seeking partial, or familial, matches. Eventually, according to one attorney, "what you're gonna end up seeing is nearly the majority of the African American population being under genetic surveillance. If you do the math, that's where you end up."

Optimism in Genomic Science

In contrast, one can fill the societal vacuum around genomics with technology optimism. Genomics research may hasten cures for cancer, heart failure, and a host of other frightening and deadly maladies; it already points to novel treatments for relatively simple genetic diseases. It may reduce particular groups' incidence of Tay Sachs disease, sickle-cell anemia, or aggressive breast cancer. Prenatal testing enables treatment of fetuses, better care for newborns, and, if needed, informed parental decisions about pregnancy termination. Individuals who learn their genomic profile can act to offset their tendency toward diabetes or heart failure or to plan for a possible debilitating disease. Life expectancy may rise with personalized medicine, and those who will benefit the most will be those who currently receive the lowest-quality health care—that is, poor people and residents of poor countries. People can find their genetic ancestry, sink roots into a particular heritage, or realize at a visceral level the meaning of the claim that racial boundaries are artificially constructed.

An optimist can go further—predicting that genomic science will overcome nutritional deficiencies and even eliminate famines by enhancing the nutrients in food. J. Craig Venter predicts that genomics will protect the environment by reducing the need for pesticides, creating oil-spill-eating bacteria, and combating climate change. Courts can use DNA evidence to reopen unsolved criminal cases, exonerate those wrongfully convicted, and come to more accurate verdicts in new cases. Here too, the most socially and racially disadvantaged Americans could reap the most benefits if genomics offsets rather than reinforc[es] racial bias in the criminal justice system. After all, as the saying goes, "genes aren't racist; people are racist."

So far, Americans are consistent optimists. Among the more than 34,600 respondents accumulated across most years since 1973 in the nationally representative General Social Survey, 43 percent express "a great deal" of confidence in "the scientific community," while only 7 percent report "hardly any confidence at all." Even more, 48 percent of the 37,000 queried since 1973, have a great deal of confidence in medicine. These are the two strongest endorsements among the thirteen institutions that have been the subjects of the GSS's repeated confidence items. In more focused questions over three decades, despite substantially different wordings, Americans have generally agreed that the benefits of genetic testing outweigh its harms. A majority expresses technology optimism about genomic science in 14 of the 20 surveys—including all since 2000—and a plurality in three more. More specifically, in all three surveys that asked this question during the 2000s, four out of five respondents agreed that medical genetic testing should be readily available "to all who want it."

Surveying Genomic Attitudes

Given these results, we start with the assumption that ordinary Americans are more likely to see benefits than dangers in genomic science—despite the fact that genomics is not well known, generates contradictory judgments from experts, has the potential for secondary effects, and rests on little previous personal experience. We explored this assumption, and its causes and effects, through an online 20-minute survey in May 2011 of 4,291 randomly selected U.S. adults, conducted by Knowledge Networks Inc. GKAP (the Survey on Genomics, Knowledge, and Policy) included 1,143 non-Hispanic whites and large oversamples of non-Hispanic African Americans (n = 1,031), non-Hispanic Asians (n = 337), self-defined non-

Hispanic multiracials (n = 635), and Hispanics (n = 1,096). Each group of respondents is weighted to represent that group in the general population, and the whole set of respondents is separately weighted to represent the American population.

GKAP focused on four genomics arenas and one scientific arena outside genomics for comparison purposes. They are, in the words of the survey items: 1) research on inherited diseases especially likely to affect people of one race or ethnicity; 2) development of genetic tests to determine an individual's likelihood of getting an inherited disease; 3) the use of DNA samples collected from patients or the general public for scientific research; 4) the use of DNA samples collected from people convicted of a serious crime for law enforcement purposes; and 5) efforts to slow or prevent global warming, sometimes termed climate change. For each arena, we asked respondents if research or activity would lead to "more good than harm," "equal amounts of harm and good," or "more harm than good" for society. Variants of this question have been used in surveys around the world, and it is our central focus in this article.

Examining the Results

GKAP respondents are more likely to say that research into all four genomics arenas will result in a net good for society than to say the reverse. . . .

Within the overall pattern, [there are] two partial exceptions. Respondents are relatively pessimistic about research on efforts to mitigate global warming, and more than usually optimistic about the use of DNA samples for law enforcement purposes. Not coincidentally, these are the two most politically charged of the five arenas.

Despite their overall technology optimism, GKAP respondents express mixed views about elites who generate or oversee genomic and other sciences. At least in these five arenas, roughly seven in ten Americans believe that scientists act in the public good; half say the same about government officials, but only two-fifths trust private companies "a lot" or "some" to act in the interests of society as a whole. Levels of trust vary a great deal according to the substantive arena under discussion. Reflecting the political controversy surrounding global warming, Americans are least likely to trust scientists, government officials, *and* private companies in that arena. Conversely, reflecting Americans' concern about crime control and just punishment, they are most likely to trust police officers and judges and juries in the arena of forensic DNA use.

Americans' optimism about genomic science and its uses is associated with backing for government involvement. At least three-fifths, and up to nine out of ten in the case of legal biobanks, endorse public funding for genomic science. Americans see no conflict between government support and government regulation, as people with strong ideological commitments on either the right or the left often do. Roughly three-fifths (four-fifths in the case of legal biobanks) want the government to regulate the same science that they also want it to fund. There can be tension between encouragement and monitoring—but most Americans do not see any such trade-off in genomic science or even in climate control.

Americans also seem willing to put their person where their mouth is. After (separately) explaining research biobanks and legal biobanks, and querying attitudes toward each, the GKAP survey asked if respondents would be "willing to contribute a DNA sample for use in current or future scientific or medical research?" or ". . . for use in current or future investigations to determine a person's guilt or innocence of a particular crime." Three-fifths reported being "somewhat willing" or "willing" to contribute in each case. . . .

The patterns in the 2011 GKAP survey show the foundation from which public opinion about genomic science may consolidate over the next few decades. If current configurations deepen and solidify, we could expect [divisions]. . . .

Despite these potentially growing divisions, a projection of GKAP results into the future encourages hopefulness (about the citizenry, if not the science). Americans' attitudes are coherent, intelligible, and largely favorable; we do not see a fearful or defensively pessimistic population in this arena. Even blacks' well-founded anxieties about forensic biobanks and mistrust of elites do not prevent 83 percent from endorsing more government funding. As one black GKAP respondent put it, "[a legal biobank] is a good instrument and tool for proving innocence or guilt." Whether that view proves naïve or prescient will take years, if not decades, to determine; in the meantime, Americans are reasonably sanguine.

"*A universal record would be a strong deterrent to first-time offenders—after all, any DNA sample left behind would be a smoking gun for the police.*"

To Stop Crime, Share Your Genes

Michael Seringhaus

A universal DNA database would be more equitable and less subject to abuses than current criminal DNA databases claims Michael Seringhaus in the following viewpoint. Although DNA does help the police solve crime, current DNA databases are racially skewed and profile even noncriminal family members. A universal DNA database would eliminate this bias and be an even stronger law enforcement tool, Seringhaus argues. Concerns about privacy are unwarranted, as the DNA used is composed mostly of biologically meaningless genetic sequences that differ enough to identify a person as unique. Seringhaus is an attorney who focuses on patent litigation with particular emphasis in the life sciences, biotechnology, and pharmaceutical fields.

As you read, consider the following questions:

1. What surprised Seringhaus about President Obama's decision to give an interview for "America's Most Wanted"?

2. How have the profiles maintained in the federal Combined DNA Index System changed, in the author's view?

3. In the author's opinion, why would universal DNA collection be fairly easy?

Perhaps the only thing more surprising than President Obama's decision to give an interview for "America's Most Wanted" last weekend [March 2010] was his apparent agreement with the program's host, John Walsh, that there should be a national DNA database with profiles of every person arrested, whether convicted or not. Many Americans feel that this proposal flies in the face of our "innocent until proven guilty" ethos, and given that African-Americans are far more likely to be arrested than whites, critics refer to such genetic collection as creating "Jim Crow's database."

Avoiding Bias

In truth, however, this is an issue where both sides are partly right. The president was correct in saying that we need a more robust DNA database, available to law enforcement in every state, to "continue to tighten the grip around folks who have perpetrated these crimes." But critics have a point that genetic police work, like the sampling of arrestees, is fraught with bias. A better solution: to keep every American's DNA profile on file.

Your sensitive genetic information would be safe. A DNA profile distills a person's complex genomic information down to a set of 26 numerical values, each characterizing the length of a certain repeated sequence of "junk" DNA that differs from person to person. Although these genetic differences are biologically meaningless—they don't correlate with any observable characteristics—tabulating the number of repeats creates a unique identifier, a DNA "fingerprint."

The genetic privacy risk from such profiling is virtually nil, because these records include none of the health and biological data present in one's genome as a whole. Aside from the ability in some cases to determine whether two individuals are closely related, DNA profiles have nothing sensitive to disclose.

But for law enforcement, the profiles are hugely important: DNA samples collected from crime scenes are compared against a standing database of profiles, and matches are investigated. Obviously, the more individuals profiled in the database, the more likely a crime-scene sample can be identified, hence the president's enthusiasm to expand the nationwide repository.

The current federal law-enforcement database, the Combined DNA Index System, or Codis, was designed for profiles of convicted criminals. When it became operational in 1998, only certain classes of convicted criminals (for instance, sex offenders) were profiled. Over the past decade, the list of qualifying crimes has quietly grown (states make their own laws on collection). And last year, the F.B.I. joined more than a dozen states and moved to include DNA profiles from arrestees not yet convicted.

There are several key problems with this approach to expanding the database. First, the national DNA database is racially skewed, as blacks and Hispanics are far more likely than whites to be convicted of crimes. Creating profiles of arrestees only adds to that imbalance.

Second, several states, including California and Colorado, have embraced a controversial new technique called familial DNA search, which exploits the fact that close relatives share substantial fractions of their DNA. If efforts to find a DNA match come up empty—that is, if the perpetrator is not yet profiled in the database—the police in these states can search for partial matches between crime-scene samples and offend-

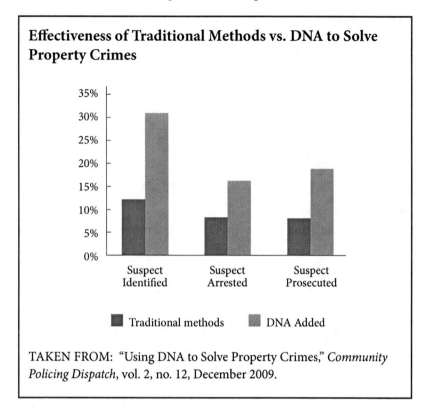

Effectiveness of Traditional Methods vs. DNA to Solve Property Crimes

TAKEN FROM: "Using DNA to Solve Property Crimes," *Community Policing Dispatch*, vol. 2, no. 12, December 2009.

ers in their record base. If they find a partial match, they can zero in on relatives of the profiled person as possible suspects.

This sounds elegant, and it occasionally works: in Britain, a handful of high-profile cases have been solved using familial search. But this approach is crippled by a very high false positive rate—many partial matches turn up people unrelated to the actual perpetrator. And it raises serious legal questions: how can we justify the de facto inclusion in DNA databases of criminals' family members who have been neither arrested nor convicted?

Moreover, familial search threatens to skew racial bias further still: by effectively including all close relatives of profiled individuals, the database could approach universal population coverage for certain races or groups and not others. Even if this bias is found to be legally permissible, it may still prove politically unpalatable.

The Benefits of a Universal Database

A much fairer system would be to store DNA profiles for each and every one of us. This would eliminate any racial bias, negate the need for the questionable technique of familial search, and of course be a far stronger tool for law enforcement than even an arrestee database.

This universal database is tenable from a privacy perspective because of the very limited information content of DNA profiles: whereas the genome itself poses a serious privacy risk, Codis-style profiles do not.

A universal record would be a strong deterrent to first-time offenders—after all, any DNA sample left behind would be a smoking gun for the police—and would enable the police to more quickly apprehend repeat criminals. It would also help prevent wrongful convictions.

As a practical matter, universal DNA collection is fairly easy: it could be done alongside blood tests on newborns, or through painless cheek swabs as a prerequisite to obtaining a driver's license or Social Security card. Once a biological sample was obtained, its use must be limited to generating a DNA profile only, and afterward the sample would be destroyed. Access to the DNA database would remain limited to law enforcement officers investigating serious crimes.

Since every American would have a stake in keeping the data private and ensuring that only the limited content vital to law enforcement was recorded, there would be far less likelihood of government misuse than in the case of a more selective database.

Provided our privacy remains secure, there is no excuse not to use every bit of science we can in the fight against crime. The key is making sure that all Americans contribute their share.

"DNA databasing . . . '[calls] into question the very meaning and possibility of human liberty.'"

DNA Databases Threaten Civil Liberties and Rights

Devon Douglas-Bowers

Laws that expand DNA collection from those convicted of increasingly less violent crimes pose a serious threat to civil liberties, claims Devon Douglas-Bowers in the following viewpoint. Although DNA is helpful in crime solving, using DNA to solve past crimes violates the Fourth Amendment prohibition against unreasonable search and seizure. In addition, Douglas-Bowers argues that because most people in the DNA database are people of color, the databank is unbalanced. Moreover, studies disprove the claim that DNA profiles deter crime. Douglas-Bowers is an independent writer and department chair of politics and government at the Hampton Institute, a think tank with a working-class perspective.

As you read, consider the following questions:

1. Of what was former American Civil Liberties Union (ACLU) associate director Barry Steinhardt skeptical concerning DNA databases?

Devon Douglas-Bowers, "Challenging Liberty: The Danger of DNA Databases," Hampton Institute, 2013. Copyright © 2013 by Hampton Institute. All rights reserved. Reproduced by permission.

2. What example does Douglas-Bowers provide of the expanding use of DNA to solve a cold case?

3. How do problems of an unbalanced DNA database expand when states permit familial DNA searches according to *Wired*?

Earlier this month [June 2013], the Supreme Court passed down a ruling stating that it is legal to take DNA swabs from arrestees without a warrant on the grounds that "a DNA cheek swab [was similar] to other common jailhouse procedures like fingerprinting;" and yesterday, it was reported that the New Jersey state senate passed a bill that "would require the collection of DNA samples from people convicted of some low-level crimes, including shoplifting and drug possession." While many are praising the passing of such legislation, it ignores the inherent dangers of allowing the government to collect DNA.

While DNA databases may seem new, this is only because they are recently coming back into the news. They have been around for quite some time as, since 1988, "every US state has established a database of criminal offenders' DNA profiles" with the goal of "quickly and accurately [matching] known offenders with crime scene evidence" [as reported in a working paper from the University of Virginia]. Politicians are arguing that taking DNA samples of criminals will actually lower crime, as the DNA works as a deterrent by increasing the likelihood that a criminal will be convicted if they are caught. However, this may not be the case, as [the] working paper from the University of Virginia found last year that, "The probability of reoffending and being convicted for any offense is 3.7 percentage points (23.4%) higher for those with a profile in the DNA database than those without," and, that DNA profiling mainly affects younger criminals with multiple convictions, as they are "85.6% more likely to be convicted of a crime within three years of release than their unprofiled counterparts." Thus, on a practical level, we should be skeptical as to whether or not DNA databases will actually lower crime in the long-term.

An Assault on Privacy

A separate but equally important issue in regards to these DNA databases is the assault on our privacy. Barry Steinhardt, then-Associate Director of the ACLU, stated back in 2000 that:

> While DNA databases may be useful to identify criminals, I am skeptical that we will ward off the temptation to expand their use. . . . In the last ten years alone, we have gone from collecting DNA only from convicted sex offenders to now including people who have been arrested but never convicted of a crime.

Indeed, Steinhardt is quite correct in that law enforcement has a history of expanding the use of their tools. One example is tasers, which, when first introduced, were seen as a way to apprehend criminals without resorting to lethal force, have now gone so far astray from that original purpose that they have been used on children. Thus, it would not be a stretch to assume that, overtime, this DNA database could be used improperly, such as in the case of Earl Whittley Davis, where his DNA was uploaded and he subsequently became a subject of a 2004 cold case murder [as reported by Candice Roman-Santos in the *Hastings Science and Technology Law Journal*]:

> Earl Whittley Davis was a shooting victim whose DNA profile was subsequently uploaded into CODIS [DNA database] even though he had done nothing wrong. This victim then became the subject of a cold case hit for a murder that occurred in 2004. Although the Maryland District Court found that crime control was a generalized interest that did not outweigh Davis' privacy when placement of his DNA profile in CODIS was not in response to a warrant or to an applicable statute, the Court held that the DNA evidence was nonetheless admissible.

The Court reasoned that placement of Davis' profile in CO-DIS was not reckless, flagrant or systematic, that exclusion would result in only marginal deterrence, if any, and that any deterrent effect would be greatly outweighed by the cost of suppressing "powerfully inculpatory and reliable DNA evidence." This case should lead people to fear that utilizing such practices to expand the DNA database would open a backdoor to population-wide data banking. By denying certiorari, the U.S. Supreme Court is implicitly affirming the rulings of the Second and Eleventh Circuits. This will make it more challenging for those opposing DNA database statutes on Fourth Amendment grounds.

In the dissenting opinion of the Supreme Court case, *Maryland v. King*, many of the Justices echoed this worry of law enforcement using the DNA databases to attempt to solve old crimes, with Justice Scalia stating, "Solving unsolved crimes is a noble objective, but it occupies a lower place in the American pantheon of noble objectives than the protection of our people from suspicionless law-enforcement searches. The Fourth Amendment must prevail."

DNA databasing is dangerous as it provides a future diary of sorts, which [an article in the *New Atlantic* says] "has the potential to reveal to third parties a person's predisposition to illnesses or behaviors without the person's knowledge; and it is permanent information, deeply personal, with predictive powers" and thus "[calls] into question the very meaning and possibility of human liberty" as it can lead into the slippery slope of pre-crime, especially with regard to a person's behaviors.

An Imbalanced Database

In addition to this, DNA databasing could negatively impact minorities and the poor, and even allow people's family members to be arrested, as *Wired* reported back in 2011:

> Civil rights advocates have warned that demographically unbalanced forensic DNA data banks could "create a feedback

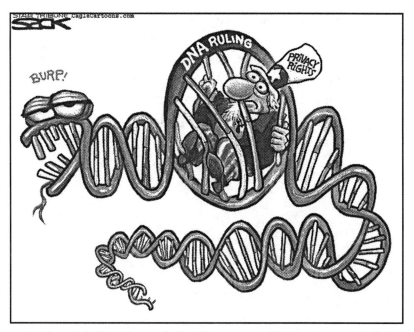

loop." Because samples are stored and compared against DNA collected at future crime scenes, police will be more likely to pursue crimes committed by members of overrepresented groups, while underrepresented groups can more easily evade detection.

The potential for problems expands when states permit so-called familial DNA searches, in which police who can't find a database match to crime scene DNA can search the database for partial matches, ostensibly from the suspect's family and relatives, who can then be targeted. It's even possible to imagine situations in which some races or groups become universally covered, while others remain only partially surveyed.

Yet, what is most worrying is the expansion of DNA databasing from major criminal offenders such as murderers and rapists to now including "some low-level crimes, including shoplifting and drug possession" [reports the *Star Ledger*].

This expansion of DNA databasing to include even victimless crimes is quite worrisome as it shows that we are moving to a state of law where virtually any crime will allow the police to draw and database one's DNA.

With the passing of this ruling and the steadily increasing implementation of DNA databasing on the state level, an ember in the light of freedom is quietly extinguished.

> "GINA now protects Americans from employer and health insurance discrimination based on genetic information, thus encouraging genetic testing and participation in research studies."

Genetic Information Non-discrimination Act

Louise Slaughter

By prohibiting employers and health insurance companies from abusing genetic information, the Genetic Information Non-discrimination Act (GINA) protects Americans from discrimination asserts Louise Slaughter in the following viewpoint. Genetic health conditions are complex, and genetic profiles are rarely predictive, yet since the completion of the Human Genome Project, some employers and insurance companies have been using the information to discriminate, according to Slaughter. GINA addresses this fundamental injustice, Slaughter argues. Not only have government agencies pursued numerous discrimination cases, she maintains, improved informed consent for the use of genetic information more effectively balances liberty and the pursuit of scientific advancement. Slaughter, who introduced GINA, represents western New York in the US House of Representatives.

Louise Slaughter, "Genetic Information Non-discrimination Act," *Harvard Journal on Legislation*, no. 50, April 1, 2009, pp. 41–48, 61–62, 66. Copyright © 2009 by the Harvard Journal on Legislation. All rights reserved. Reproduced by permission.

As you read, consider the following questions:

1. According to Slaughter, why are lawmakers challenged by genomic legislation?

2. What did a 1996 Genetic Alliance study find?

3. What is the two-fold intent of GINA, in Slaughter's view?

In 1995, the year I first introduced legislation to address genetic discrimination, the genomic era was still in its burgeoning stages. The human genome had not yet been fully sequenced, and the potential for personalized medicine had not yet been realized. The future for advances in genomic-based medicine held both promise and trepidation for the American people. Surveys showed that while "[t]he majority of Americans enthusiastically support[ed] genetic testing for research and health care ... a large majority (92%) also express[ed] concern that results of a genetic test could be used in ways that are harmful." Evidence was mounting that Americans were already subjected to genetic discrimination, and without protective legislative action, their ranks would only grow. Furthermore, due to fear of discrimination, people shied away from participation in research studies—the very research that could benefit human health.

At the time, no federal laws addressed discrimination based on genetic information in a comprehensive fashion. While certain federal statutes protected specific types of health and personal information, substantial gaps and inconsistencies remained with respect to genetic discrimination by health insurers and employers. In order to encourage the tremendous potential of genomic medicine for rapid advancement in technology and human health, Congress needed to pass legislation to protect the rights of citizens. As Thomas Jefferson so aptly stated in 1816, in a quote that is now inscribed on the Jefferson Memorial in Washington, D.C.:

Laws and institutions must go hand in hand with the progress of the human mind. As that becomes more developed, more enlightened, as new discoveries are made, new truths disclosed, and manners and opinions change with the change of circumstances, institutions must advance also, and keep pace with the times.

Given the exponential progress of genomic technology and discovery, keeping pace with the times was a growing challenge for lawmakers, who are most often not equipped with a background in the advanced science of genetics. Such limitations in knowledge had to be bridged in order to make informed policy decisions. In addition, competing interests on the part of health insurance companies and businesses posed significant challenges in building support for legislation on genetic information. For these reasons, I championed GINA for thirteen years. It was a long and arduous process, but ultimately successful. GINA now protects Americans from employer and health insurance discrimination based on genetic information, thus encouraging genetic testing and participation in research studies.

Genomic Research and Genetic Tests

The Human Genome Project ("HGP") was first proposed to Congress in 1990 by the Department of Energy ("DOE") and the National Institutes of Health ("NIH") as part of an ambitious interagency endeavor to map and sequence the complete human genome. It was hoped that by sequencing and characterizing the genome we would further our understanding of human genetics, as well as the role of genes in health and disease. The results from this project were expected to shape the future of biological and biomedical research.

Even before the completion of the HGP, scientists had made great advances in genetic research, identifying more than 6,000 single-gene disorders, or diseases caused by a single genetic mutation, including cystic fibrosis, sickle cell anemia,

Huntington's disease, and muscular dystrophy. A number of genetic tests were available that could provide individuals with information about their likelihood of contracting a disease or developing a health condition. For example, Huntington's disease is passed from parent to child through a genetic mutation or misspelling of a normal gene. This genetic mutation is dominant, which means that if an individual carries just one copy of the defective gene, that person will contract the neurodegenerative disorder. It also means that any child of an affected person has a 50% chance of inheriting the disease.

However, most genetic-based health conditions are not so straightforward. As researchers have learned over the years, disease is rarely a simple gene-to-symptom phenomenon. Instead it is often the result of complex interactions of many different genes as well as environmental factors. Carrying a given genetic mutation does not guarantee that one will fall ill; a genetic flaw simply confers a level of higher or lower risk upon the carrier. Moreover, our limited understanding of genetic risk and its interplay with other factors, such as environmental exposures that may either increase risk or protect against it, make it exceedingly difficult to predict with certainty what a given genetic defect means for an individual. Fully understanding how the genome affects human health will take much future work.

After thirteen years of work and $3 billion of investment, sequencing of the human genome was completed in 2003—fifty years after the publication of Watson and Crick's seminal 1953 paper on the structure of the DNA double-helix, the molecule that encodes genetic information from one generation to the next. Completion of the HGP may very well be the most momentous medical achievement in this century, with unparalleled implications for public health and modern medicine. Researchers are now using this wealth of data to link genetic markers to human diseases and health conditions, help-

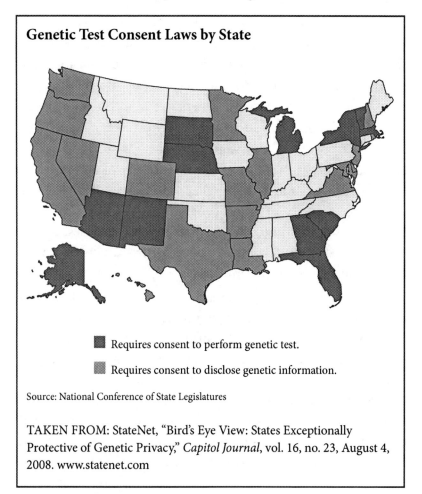

Genetic Test Consent Laws by State

■ Requires consent to perform genetic test.

■ Requires consent to disclose genetic information.

Source: National Conference of State Legislatures

TAKEN FROM: StateNet, "Bird's Eye View: States Exceptionally Protective of Genetic Privacy," *Capitol Journal*, vol. 16, no. 23, August 4, 2008. www.statenet.com

ing to guide diagnoses as well as treatment and prevention strategies. And this is only the beginning.

Genetic Discrimination and Public Perception

Each of us is thought to carry dozens of glitches in our DNA. Single-gene disorders alone are estimated to occur in 1 out of every 200 births. Complex genetic disorders such as heart disease, high blood pressure, Alzheimer's disease, cancer, and diabetes represent the majority of the 15,500 recognized genetic disorders afflicting 13 million Americans. Given the prevalence of genetic mutations, any one of us could have a predisposition for a genetic disorder. The availability of genetic tests for some of these predispositions has clear benefits for treatment and prevention strategies. Despite the uncertainties and complexities that come with genetic testing, this information was also of great interest to third parties such as employers and health insurers, who were concerned about the negative effects of genetic diseases on the productivity of employees or the cost for treatment of beneficiaries. Surveys showed that while the majority of Americans enthusiastically supported genetic testing for research and health care purposes, a large majority (92%) also expressed concerns that results of genetic tests could be used in harmful ways.

Opponents of Congressional action to address this problem argued that legislation was premature given that genetic discrimination was relatively infrequent. I would argue that even a rare discrimination event should not happen, and cases had already been documented. In the 1970s, African-Americans were targeted for genetic testing for sickle cell disease, a genetic blood disorder. Test results were not kept confidential and led to stigmatization and discrimination by employers and health insurance companies. In 1998, a court ruled that Lawrence-Berkeley Laboratories had violated the privacy rights of its employees by performing tests for syphilis, sickle cell genetic markers, and pregnancy without their knowledge or consent over a twenty-five-year period. In 2000, Gary Avary, an employee of the Burlington Northern Santa Fe Railroad, discovered that his employer had administered genetic tests for carpal tunnel predisposition on employees without their knowledge or consent. The U.S. Equal Employment Opportunity Commission ("EEOC") settled this case in court by challenging the use of workplace genetic testing under the Americans with Disabilities Act of 1990 ("ADA"). Speaking of his experience, Mr. Avary stated that:

What happened to me should not happen to anyone, especially in the United States. It is a direct infringement on our fundamental right to be who we are. No one can help how they are put together, only God knows that. The employer, the insurance company or anyone else has no business of that knowledge. That information . . . should not be used against you and your family for hiring and firing practices, or acceptance and/or denial into insurance programs.

These examples are only a handful of the dozens of genetic discrimination cases that had been documented. A study in 1996 by the Genetic Alliance, a coalition of more than 600 special interest groups, found that thirteen percent of respondents reported that they believed they or relatives had been denied jobs or dismissed from them because of genetic conditions. Such perceived abuses fed a growing public fear of genetic discrimination, leading many Americans to forgo genetic testing even if early detection of a genetic predisposition could have provided beneficial health information. Even a majority of genetic counselors surveyed—those well-versed in the policies and protections of the law—reported they would not bill their insurance companies for a genetic test due to fear of discrimination. Twenty-six percent responded that they would use an alias to obtain a genetic test so as to reduce the risk of discrimination and maximize confidentiality. Such fears were not unsubstantiated. A 2007 study on medical underwriting indicated that a percentage of health insurance applicants were denied coverage, administered a surcharge on premiums, or given limited coverage benefits based on genetic information.

Genetic discrimination is not acceptable in the United States. No one should be stigmatized or discriminated against because of genetic predispositions that we all may carry. People should be free to know their own genetic predisposition to diseases for purposes of early treatment and lifestyle changes such as diet, exercise, or changes in environment, without being concerned that they will be discriminated against based on this information. As Francis Collins, leader of the HGP and now Director of the National Institutes of Health, stated, "Genetic information and genetic technology . . . can be used in ways that are fundamentally unjust. . . . Already . . . people have lost their jobs, lost their health insurance, and lost their economic well-being . . . due to the unfair and inappropriate use of genetic information."

However, without protections in place, there is always a risk that individuals will be discriminated against by their employer or insurance company. The idea of legislation creating such protections was supported by the general public. A 2004 survey indicated that eighty percent of respondents opposed allowing health insurers access to their genetic information. Over ninety percent of respondents felt that employers should not have access to this information. According to a 2006 survey by Cogent Research, seventy-two percent of Americans agreed that the government should establish laws and regulations to protect the privacy of individuals' genetic information, and eighty-five percent said that without amending current law, employers would use this information to discriminate among employees.

Clearly, there was a need and public will for measures to be taken to protect the basic rights of every American. For life-saving scientific advances to continue and for the potential of genome technology to be fully realized, genetic testing had to be something commonplace rather than something feared. The promise of genomics is in jeopardy if our laws fail to adequately protect citizens from abuse and misuses of genetic information. . . .

Congressional action was needed to create comprehensive legislation to address gaps at the state and federal level in order to ensure against the discrimination of individuals on the basis of genetic information. GINA was straightforward, commonsense, and necessary legislation to protect Americans from discrimination. . . .

Assessing the Impact

The intent of GINA was two-fold: to prohibit discrimination based on genetic information and to encourage genetic testing and participation in genetic research studies. In passing legislation as a largely preventive measure, the impact of GINA on genetic discrimination was obscured by its own success. At the time of enactment, studies documenting genetic discrimination had not been implemented on a systemic level. There also is no baseline data indicating the rates at which individuals declined to participate in genetic testing or clinical trials due to the fear of discrimination, so we cannot report on a change in this behavior related to the passage of GINA. Under these circumstances, it is extremely difficult to determine whether GINA has reduced or prevented cases of genetic discrimination.

We do, however, have enforcement data from the EEOC. For 2010–2011, the EEOC found reasonable cause to believe genetic discrimination has occurred in 143 cases, and a half million dollars has been awarded in damages in 2011–2012. In my opinion, these statistics are certainly evidence of success of the law.

Furthermore, we know that practice has changed for investigators performing research studies that include genetic testing. The Department of Health and Human Services put out GINA guidance for investigators and Institutional Review Boards in 2009 that suggests including the following information in informed consent agreements that participants read and sign prior to enrolling in research studies:

A new Federal law, called the Genetic Information Nondiscrimination Act (GINA), generally makes it illegal for health insurance companies, group health plans, and most employers to discriminate against you based on your genetic information. This law generally will protect you in the following ways:

- Health insurance companies and group health plans may not request your genetic information that we get from this research.

- Health insurance companies and group health plans may not use your genetic information when making decisions regarding your eligibility or premiums.

- Employers with 15 or more employees may not use your genetic information that we get from this research when making a decision to hire, promote, or fire you or when setting the terms of your employment.

All health insurance companies and group health plans must follow this law by May 21, 2010. All employers with 15 or more employees must follow this law as of November 21, 2009. Be aware that this new Federal law does not protect you against genetic discrimination by companies that sell life insurance, disability insurance, or long-term care insurance.

Having this knowledge prior to participating in research should assuage many of the fears that previously prevented people from participating in research. I believe that we can point to the rapid advancement in personalized medicine and the myriad other advances in genetics and genomics as evidence that sufficient participation is taking place, just as we hoped to foster by passing this bill. . . .

Conclusion

The sequencing of the human genome held great promise for human health, but at the same time held great potential for stigmatization and discrimination. As Senator Jeffords and Senator Daschle once rightly stated, "Without adequate safeguards, the genetic revolution could mean one step forward for science and two steps backwards for civil rights." Indeed, GINA has done more than stamp out a new form of discrimination. It has helped our country become a leader in the field of genomic research, and helped us realize the tremendous potential of scientific advancement without jeopardizing our fundamental right to privacy.

When GINA passed in 2008, the late Senator Kennedy (D-Mass.) declared it the "first civil rights bill of the new century." This momentous event was the culmination of a dedicated systematic and bipartisan effort. Members on both sides of the aisle were committed to moving this bill forward. . . . I will forever be grateful to these individuals and their dedicated staff for taking on this battle with me.

In this business, you're never defeated until you give up—and I never give up. GINA took thirteen long years to pass the House and Senate and get signed into law. I consider it one of my greatest achievements as a member of Congress. I am proud of the potential it offers to advance medical research and treatment by freeing people from the fear of losing their job or health insurance based on genetic information. As with all incremental advances in civil rights, the fight must continue and more must be done. I look forward to the continued challenge of protecting American citizens.

> "The worst thing that could happen is for advocates of genetic rights and fairness in health care to be satisfied with GINA or exult in its enactment."

The Genetic Information Non-discrimination Act Does Not Protect Americans from Genetic Discrimination

Mark A. Rothstein

Lawmakers enacted the Genetic Information Non-discrimination Act (GINA) to encourage Americans to participate in genetic research—not protect against growing genetic discrimination— argues Mark A. Rothstein in the following viewpoint. In truth, GINA offers Americans little protection, as it only protects against discrimination in employment and health insurance situations and applies only to those who show no symptoms. Once people develop the disease, they have little protection, Rothstein claims. Moreover, GINA's employment provisions are ineffective as employers may legally obtain medical records; however, separating genetic from medical information does pose significant chal-

Mark A. Rothstein, "GINA's Beauty Is Only Skin Deep," *GeneWatch*, vol. 22, no. 2, 209. Reprinted with the permission of GeneWatch, the magazine of the Council for Responsible Genetics.

lenges. Rothstein is chair of law and medicine and director of the Institute for Bioethics, Health Policy, and Law at the University of Louisville School of Medicine.

As you read, consider the following questions:

1. How long did it take to pass GINA?

2. In what types of transactions does GINA do nothing to prohibit discrimination?

3. In Rothstein's opinion, under what circumstances would GINA be valuable?

It is hard to be critical of the Genetic Information Nondiscrimination Act of 2008 (GINA). After all, it's the first federal law enacted to prohibit genetic discrimination, and passing it took 13 years of work by people whose goals I share. In analyzing the law, however, it is apparent that GINA fails to resolve or even address many of the basic concerns that drove the legislative effort. It is also clear why, despite 13 years of wrangling on Capitol Hill, the final version of GINA was passed unanimously in the Senate and received only one negative vote in the House of Representatives—and that from inveterate naysayer, Representative Ron Paul.

Assuaging Real Fears

GINA was *not* enacted in response to a wave of genetic discrimination, defined as the adverse treatment of an individual based on genotype. There have been very few documented cases of such discrimination. To some degree, GINA was enacted to prevent genetic discrimination in the future when health records will routinely contain genetic information and genetic testing will be so inexpensive that it's cost-effective to perform it on a widespread basis. The real reason for enacting GINA was to assure people that they could undergo genetic testing without fear of genetic discrimination. As any clinical geneticist or genetic counselor will tell you, these fears are real.

According to section 2(5) of GINA, federal legislation "is necessary to fully protect the public from discrimination and allay their concerns about the potential for discrimination, thereby allowing individuals to take advantage of genetic testing, technologies, research, and new therapies." The phrase "fully protect the public" is a curious choice of wording. GINA *did* extend protection against genetic discrimination to the few states that had not previously enacted a law prohibiting genetic discrimination in health insurance or the one-third of the states without a law banning genetic discrimination in employment. Yet, the method of protection, similar to state approaches, is not fully protective in any way. Therefore, it would be more accurate to say that GINA "fully covers" the public; it certainly does not provide "full protection."

Examining GINA's Flaws

There are three major flaws with GINA. First, it applies only to two aspects of the problem, discrimination in health insurance and employment. To allay public concerns about genetic discrimination, it's necessary to prohibit the adverse treatment of individuals in numerous settings. GINA does nothing to prohibit discrimination in life insurance, disability insurance, long-term care insurance, mortgages, commercial transactions, or any of the other possible uses of genetic information. It remains to be seen whether GINA's limited applicability, coupled with its inadequate protections in health insurance and employment, will be enough to reassure the public that undergoing genetic testing will not endanger their economic security.

Second, GINA's prohibition on genetic discrimination in health insurance is largely a mirage. The Health Insurance Portability and Accountability Act (HIPAA) contains a little-known provision prohibiting employer-sponsored group health plans from denying individuals coverage, charging them higher rates, or varying their coverage based on "genetic information." Significantly, HIPAA prohibits discrimination by group health plans on the basis of *any* health information. Because HIPAA prohibits genetic discrimination for the largest source of private health coverage (group plans), GINA's main value is to cover people with individual health insurance policies in the few states that did not previously enact a state genetic nondiscrimination law.

Limited Application

Unfortunately, the protections afforded individuals under either state laws prohibiting genetic discrimination in health insurance or GINA are not particularly robust or valuable. (Because state laws and GINA are similar in substance, for simplicity, I'll merely refer to GINA.) The problem is that GINA only applies to asymptomatic individuals. There are few incentives for health insurers to discriminate against asymptomatic individuals and few laws to prohibit them from discriminating against symptomatic individuals.

An example will bring this problem more clearly into focus. Under GINA, it is unlawful for an individual health insurance company to refuse [to] offer coverage, charge higher rates, or exclude certain conditions on the basis of genetic information, including the results of a genetic test. For example, it would be unlawful to deny coverage to a woman with a positive test for one of the breast cancer mutations. Now, suppose some months or years later, the woman develops breast cancer. GINA simply does not apply. The insurance company's permissible response would depend on state insurance law. In virtually every state, the health insurance company could lawfully react to the changed health status of the individual by refusing to renew the policy (at its typical annual renewal date), increase the rates to reflect the increased risk (and the rates might double or triple), or renew the policy but exclude coverage for breast cancer.

GINA does have some limited value in this scenario. Because of GINA an at-risk woman is no worse off in terms of insurability due to having a genetic test, and there might be psychological or medical benefits from being tested, depending on the results. Yet, the overall picture in terms of health policy remains bleak. So long as individual health insurance is medically underwritten at the initial application and for renewals, individuals who are ill or more likely to become ill are extremely vulnerable. Many advocates and policy makers have concentrated on the issue of genetic discrimination in health insurance, but the issue is much broader and cannot be resolved by such a narrow focus. To state the obvious: Under any system of universal access to health care, the issue of genetic discrimination in health insurance disappears.

Ineffective Employment Provisions

Third, the employment provisions of GINA are ineffective, but for different reasons. As with health insurance, the employment provisions only apply to individuals who are asymptomatic. The Americans with Disabilities Act (ADA) covers individuals who have substantially limiting impairments and therefore the ADA would prohibit discrimination against symptomatic individuals, regardless of the cause of their condition.

GINA makes it unlawful for an employer to request, require, or purchase genetic information regarding an applicant or employee. This is an important issue, because individuals are concerned with employers merely having access to their genetic information. The problem is that the provision is infeasible and therefore is not being followed.

Under the ADA after a conditional offer of employment, it is lawful for an employer to require individuals to undergo a preplacement medical examination and to sign an authorization releasing all of their medical records to the employer. In effect, GINA now qualifies this by saying that employers can require the release of all medical information except genetic information. GINA defines genetic information as the genetic tests of the individual, genetic tests of the individual's family members, and family health histories. Because this information is commonly interspersed in medical records there is no practical way for the custodians of the health records (e.g., physicians, hospitals) to send only non-genetic information. In practice, when presented with a limited or unlimited request, the custodians usually send the entire records.

The development and adoption of electronic health records (EHRs) and networks hold the possibility of using health information technology to limit the scope of health information disclosed for any particular purpose. Unfortunately, there have been no efforts undertaken to design health records with the capacity to segment or sequester sensitive health information (including but not limited to genetic information) to facilitate more targeted access or disclosures. Without such efforts, health privacy will decline precipitously with the shift to EHRs because records increasingly will be comprehensive (i.e., containing information generated by substantially all health care providers) and longitudinal (i.e., containing information over an extended period of time). Thus, when employers and other third parties require access to an individual's health records the amount of information they receive will be much more extensive than they receive today.

Halfway Measures

GINA represents an incremental approach to problems that do not lend themselves to incremental approaches. Numerous entities have economic interests in learning about an individual's current or likely future health. GINA consists of halfway measures limited to health insurance and employment that do not provide adequate assurances to the public that genetic information will not be used to their detriment in other ways. GINA prohibits genetic discrimination in individual health insurance against people when they are asymptomatic, but fails to provide them with what they need most—health coverage when they are ill. GINA prohibits employers from requesting or requiring the release of genetic information in comprehensive health records at a time when it is infeasible to separate genetic information from other health records.

If GINA serves to declare the unacceptability of genetic-based discrimination and begins a process of careful consideration of a wide range of health related issues, then it will be valuable. But it is far from clear that GINA will have such an effect. It is not clear that GINA, by singling out genetic information for special treatment, will not increase the stigma associated with genetics and encourage other condition-specific, rather than comprehensive, legislation. It is not clear whether GINA will be the first step to meaningful legislation or cause legislative fatigue based on the erroneous assumption that the issues already had been resolved. It is not clear whether consumers will understand GINA's limitations or mistakenly rely on its presumed protections. In the short term, the worst thing that could happen is for advocates of genetic rights and fairness in health care to be satisfied with GINA or exult in its enactment.

Periodical and Internet Sources Bibliography

The following articles have been selected to supplement the diverse views presented in this chapter.

Ronald Bailey	"Fight Crime with a Universal DNA Database?" *Reason*, March 17, 2010.
John Branton	"DNA Database Helping to Solve More Crimes," *Seattle Times*, February 23, 2011.
Diane Diamond	"Searching the Family DNA Tree," *Huffington Post*, April 12, 2011.
Dov Fox	"The Future of Genetic Privacy," *Huffington Post*, August 13, 2013.
Henry T. Greely	"Time to Raise Some Hell," *GeneWatch*, February/March 2011.
Gina Kolata	"Poking Holes in Genetic Privacy," *New York Times*, June 16, 2013.
Scot Lemieux	"Are Police Building a Massive DNA Database?" *AlterNet*, March 23, 2012.
Caroline Perry	"Ethics and Genetics in the Digital Age," *Harvard Gazette*, April 21, 2011.
Lorelei E. Walker and Mark A. Rothstein	"Are Genetic Discrimination Laws Up to the Task?" *Medscape*, August 8, 2012.
Carly Weeks	"Health Insurance and 'Genetic Discrimination': Are Rules Needed?" *Globe and Mail (Canada)*, January 1, 2012.
Christy White	"Genetic Privacy Worries on the Rise," *GeneWatch*, February/March 2011.

For Further Discussion

Chapter 1

1. Scott Kirsner asserts that gene therapies are showing signs of promise in treating debilitating diseases. Timothy Caulfield argues that continued claims that human genetic knowledge will revolutionize medicine do more harm than good. Identify the types of evidence the authors use to support their arguments. Which type of evidence do you find more persuasive? Explain.

2. Janet Rowley supports embryonic stem cell research, arguing that with oversight, scientists can conduct research using embryonic stem cells to better understand life-threatening diseases while preserving human dignity. Michael Cook counters that fruitless research using embryonic stem cells is unnecessary as researchers have had more success with adult cells. How do the authors' ethical views about research using embryonic stem cells differ, and how do these views inform their rhetoric? Which rhetorical strategy do you find more persuasive?

3. Heather Long fears that if parents are able to select genetic traits to ensure a healthy embryo, some will inevitably choose traits unrelated to health that give their children an advantage, creating a genetic elite. Will Oremus does not dispute that some parents would likely use genetic selection to improve their children's intelligence or appearance. He claims, however, that the ability to select these traits is distant. How does the fact that scientists will not have—in the near future—a clear understanding of the complex relationship between genes and the environment and the related impact on traits such as intelligence affect which viewpoint you find more persuasive? Does

agreeing with one view necessarily mean you must disagree with the other? Explain.

4. Both John Naish and Theodore Friedmann agree that athletes and their trainers and doctors will likely pursue genetic doping to improve athletic performance. However, Naish is concerned about the challenge of detecting gene doping while Friedmann explores the safety concerns and whether gene doping will even work. Note the affiliations of the authors. How do the affiliations influence each author's rhetoric? Which do you find more persuasive? Explain.

5. Of the genetic enhancements and therapies explored in this chapter, which do you think will be most beneficial? Which do you think poses the greatest risk, if any? Explain.

Chapter 2

1. Lawrence Horn and Kristin Neuman claim that genetic patents promote scientific and medical innovation because patents promise a potential return on genetic research, which requires significant investment. Robin Abcarian, on the other hand, believes that patents on human genes create a monopoly on something that occurs naturally and prevents others from pursuing useful genetic developments. Note the affiliations of the authors. How do the affiliations influence each author's rhetoric? Which do you find more persuasive? Explain.

2. Sharon Levy argues that the US Supreme Court decision in *Association for Molecular Pathology v. Myriad Genetics* will stifle genetic research. Ed Mannino disagrees, claiming the court balanced the need to promote innovation while preventing patent practices that inhibit competition. Identify the types of evidence the authors use to support their arguments. Which type of evidence do you find more persuasive and why?

3. What commonalities among the evidence and rhetoric can you find in the viewpoints on both sides of the debate in this chapter? What impact do these strategies have on the viewpoints' persuasiveness? Explain.

Chapter 3

1. Arthur Caplan believes that many consumers do not benefit from the information in direct-to-consumer genetic tests, which are often inaccurate. Ricki Lewis comes to the opposite conclusion. Both Caplan and Lewis are professors of bioethics, yet each draws different conclusions. How does this illuminate ethical debates about human genetics? Which author do you find more persuasive? Explain how your choice is informed by the author's rhetoric.

2. Harriet Hall opposes direct-to-consumer tests for some of the same reasons as Caplan; however, she adds that the real promise is in research—not testing. Unlike Lewis and Caplan, Hall is a retired physician who opposes quackery and writes for *Skeptic Magazine*. How does her affiliation influence her rhetoric? Explain.

3. Marilynn Marchione maintains that modern prenatal genetic tests are less risky and give women more information about their pregnancies. Kristan Hawkins argues that prenatal genetic testing promotes abortion. Carolyn Y. Johnson worries that parental genetic testing will change how people define what a normal baby is. None of these authors is a geneticist, ethicist, or physician. Moreover, each author's rhetoric is quite different. How does each author's rhetoric and the evidence each provides influence which viewpoint you think is most and least persuasive? Explain.

Chapter 4

1. Philip L. Bereano identifies several threats to civil liberties posed by the collection of human genetic information.

According to Jennifer Hochschild, Alex Crabill, and Maya Sen, however, Americans are, nevertheless, optimistic about its benefits. In their analysis, Hochschild, Crabill, and Sen note, however, that nonexperts are not always able to accurately assess the dangers—which, some claim, explains American optimism. These authors also note that this optimism impacts policy. Would the concerns expressed by Bereano be adequate to bridge the genetic knowledge gap and make Americans less optimistic, or is their optimism defensible? Explain.

2. Michael Seringhaus claims that a universal DNA database is the best way to fairly use DNA evidence in crime solving. Devon Douglas-Bowers believes that DNA databases pose a serious threat to civil liberties, especially for minorities. Would Seringhaus's universal DNA database address Douglas-Bowers's concerns about the impact on minorities? What about his Fourth Amendment concerns? What impact does the evidence each author provides have on your conclusions? Explain.

3. Louise Slaughter, who introduced the Genetic Information Non-discrimination Act (GINA) to the US House of Representatives, asserts that it effectively protects against discrimination. Mark A. Rothstein argues, however, that its protection is limited. Moreover, he claims, Congress passed it to promote participation in genetic research—not to protect against discrimination. Both authors believe that protection against discrimination on the basis of genetic information is necessary. In what other issues do the authors appear to agree or disagree? Does agreeing with one view necessarily mean you must disagree with the other? Explain.

4. What commonalities among the evidence and rhetoric can you find in the viewpoints on both sides of the debate in this chapter? What impact do these strategies have on the viewpoints' persuasiveness? Explain.

Organizations to Contact

The editors have compiled the following list of organizations concerned with the issues debated in this book. The descriptions are derived from materials provided by the organizations. All have publications or information available for interested readers. The list was compiled on the date of publication of the present volume; names, addresses, phone and fax numbers, and email and Internet addresses may change. Be aware that many organizations take several weeks or longer to respond to inquiries, so allow as much time as possible.

Alliance for Regenerative Medicine (ARM)
525 Second Street NE, Washington, DC   20002
(202) 568-6240
e-mail: info@alliancerm.org
website: http://alliancerm.org

ARM advances regenerative medicine by representing, supporting, and engaging all stakeholders, including companies, academic research institutions, patient advocacy groups, foundations, health insurers, and financial institutions. Fact sheets on issues surrounding genomic medicine, including its promise and potential, clinical trials, and clinical milestones, are available on its website.

American Civil Liberties Union (ACLU)
125 Broad Street, 18th Floor, New York, NY   10004
(212) 549-2500
website: www.aclu.org

The ACLU works to uphold civil rights and liberties, focusing on rights such as free speech, equal protection, due process, and privacy. ACLU court cases address and define these civil rights and liberties, and, in recent years, many ACLU court cases have specifically addressed gene patent and genetic privacy issues. Special feature articles, infographics, and videos on gene patents and genetic privacy are available on the ACLU's website, including an electronic copy of the Supreme Court decision in *Association for Molecular Pathology v. Myriad Genetics.*

Biotechnology Industry Organization (BIO)

1225 Eye Street NW, Suite 400, Washington, DC   20005
(202) 962-9200 • fax: (202) 962-9201
e-mail: biomember@bio.org
website: www.bio.org

BIO represents biotechnology companies, academic institutions, state biotechnology centers, and related organizations that support the use of biotechnology in improving health care, agriculture, efforts to clean up the environment, and other fields. BIO works to educate the public about biotechnology and respond to concerns about the safety of genetic technologies. It publishes articles such as "The Value of Therapeutic Cloning for Patients" and the brochure "Bioethics: Facing the Future Responsibly," which are available on its website.

Center for Bioethics and Human Dignity (CBHD)

2065 Half Day Road, Bannockburn, IL   60015
(847) 317-8180 • fax: (847) 317-8153
e-mail: info@cbhd.org
website: www.cbhd.org

CBHD is an international education center established to bring Christian perspectives to bear on contemporary bioethical challenges facing society. Its publications address genetic technologies as well as other topics such as euthanasia and abortion. It publishes the quarterly *Dignitas*. Articles published on its website include "From Personalized Medicine to Consumer-Driven Testing: An Update on Direct-to-Consumer Genetic Tests," "Genetic Testing: Ethics, Regulation, and Online Accessibility," and "Who Will Be the Last Human? Or, Are We Even Still Human?"

Center for Genetics and Society (CGS)

1936 University Ave., Suite 350, Berkeley, CA   94704
(510) 625-0819 • fax: (510) 665-8760
e-mail: info@geneticsandsociety.org
website: www.geneticsandsociety.org

CGS is a nonprofit public-information group that promotes the responsible use of gene technologies. The center supports benign and beneficent medical applications of human genetic and reproductive technologies and opposes applications that objectify and commodify human life and threaten to divide human society. On its website, CGS publishes the *Biopolitical Times* blog, articles, reports, multimedia, fact sheets, talks, and testimonies, as well as the op-eds: "Your Body, Their Property" and "A Slippery Slope to Human Germline Modification." Additionally, CGS publishes "Human Embryonic Stem Cell Research: Frequently Asked Questions and Fact Sheet" and the report, *Playing the Gene Card?*

Council for Responsible Genetics (CRG)

5 Upland Road, Suite 3, Cambridge, MA   02140
(617) 868-0870 • fax: (617) 491-5344
e-mail: crg@gene-watch.org
website: www.gene-watch.org

CRG is a national nonprofit organization of scientists, public health advocates, and others who promote a comprehensive public interest agenda for biotechnology. Its members work to raise public awareness about genetic discrimination, patenting life forms, food safety, and environmental quality. CRG publishes *GeneWatch* magazine, providing access to current and archived articles on its website.

Genetic Alliance

4301 Connecticut Ave. NW, Suite 404
Washington, DC   20008-2369
(202) 966-5557 • fax: (202) 966-8553
e-mail: info@geneticalliance.org
website: www.geneticalliacne.org

Genetic Alliance is a coalition of disease-advocacy groups that presses for better translation of gene science into diagnostics and therapies. Its network also includes universities, private companies, government agencies, and public policy organizations. It publishes the monthly peer-reviewed journal *Genetic Testing and Molecular Biomarkers*, a weekly bulletin of current advances, new alliances, and policy concerns, and help guides such as *How Do I talk to My Family About My Genetic Condition?* and *Making Sense of Your Genes: A Guide to Genetic Counseling.*

The Hastings Center
21 Malcolm Gordon Road, Garrison, NY   10524-5555
(845) 424-4040 • fax: (845) 424-4545
e-mail: mail@thehastingscenter.org
website: www.thehastingscenter.org

The Hastings Center is an independent research institute that explores the medical, ethical, and social ramifications of biomedical advances. The center publishes books, including *Reprogenetics*, the bimonthly *Hastings Center Report*, and the bimonthly newsletter *IRB: Ethics & Human Research.*

National Breast Cancer Coalition
1101 17th Street NW, Suite 1300, Washington, DC   20036
(202) 296-7477 • fax: (202) 265-6854
website: www.breastcancerdeadline2020.org

National Breast Cancer Coalition is a grassroots advocacy organization working to improve public policies on breast cancer research and treatment. Its goal is to end breast cancer by January 1, 2020. On its website, it publishes "A Blueprint for Breast Cancer Deadline 2020," breast cancer fact sheets, its 2013 progress report, and links to current articles on issues related to breast cancer.

National Human Genome Research Institute (NHGRI)
9000 Rockville Pike, Bethesda, MD   20892
(301) 402-0911 • fax: (301) 402-2218
website: www.genome.gov

The National Institutes of Health (NIH) is the federal government's primary agency for the support of biomedical research. As a division of NIH, NHGRI's mission was to head the Human Genome Project, the federally funded effort to map all human genes, which was completed in April 2003. Now, NHGRI has moved into the genomic arena, with research aimed at improving human health and fighting disease. Information on the project and relevant articles are available on its website.

Public Patent Foundation
Benjamin Cardozo School of Law, New York, NY   10003
(212) 545-5337 • fax: (212) 591-6038
email: info@pubpat.org
website: www.pubpat.org

The Public Patent Foundation is a nonprofit legal services organization working to limit abuse in the US patent system. It believes that some patents make products too expensive for consumers, prevent other scientists from advancing technology, hurt small business, and restrain civil liberties and freedoms. On its website, it publishes news on current patent cases, including gene patents, links to its cases, and public information videos, articles, speeches, and presentations.

Stanford University Center for Biomedical Ethics (SCBE)
701 Welch Road, Building A, Suite 1105
Palo Alto, CA   94305-5417
(650) 723-5760 • fax: (650) 725-6131
email: SCBE-info@med.stanford.edu
website: http://scbe.stanford.edu

SCBE engages in interdisciplinary research on moral questions arising from the complex relationships among medicine, science, and society. It is committed to exploring and promoting compassionate approaches to the practice of medicine in a climate of socioeconomic and technological change. One of its programs is the Center for Integration of Research on Genetics and Ethics (CIRGE). On the CIRGE link, it publishes recent issues of its newsletter and articles on genetic ethics, including "Attitudes Towards Social Networking and Sharing Behaviors Among Consumers of Direct-to-Consumer Personal Genomics" and "Can Informed Consent Go Too Far? Balancing Consent and Public Benefit in Research."

US Patent and Trademark Office (USPTO)
600 Dulany Street, Alexandria, VA   22314
(571) 272-1000
website: www.uspto.gov

USPTO is the federal agency for granting US patents and registering trademarks, fulfilling the mandate of Article I, Section 8, Clause 8, of the US Constitution to: "promote the progress of science and the useful arts by securing for limited times to inventors the exclusive right to their respective discoveries." USPTO advises the president of the United States, the secretary of commerce, and US government agencies on intellectual property (IP) policy, protection, and enforcement; and promotes stronger and more effective IP protection around the world. On its website, USPTO provides access to fact sheets on how to file patents and trademarks as well as current information on IP law and policy. The USPTO website also includes the recent year's *Official Gazette for Patents* and *Official Gazette for Trademarks*, a weekly journal of patents granted and trademarks published. It also publishes current press releases, videos, speeches, and testimony.

Bibliography of Books

Nick Bostrom and Julian Savulescu, eds.   *Human Enhancement.* New York: Oxford University Press, 2008.

Michael K. Danquah and Ram I. Mahato, eds.   *Emerging Trends in Cell and Gene Therapy.* New York: Humana, 2013.

Dena Davis   *Genetic Dilemmas: Reproductive Technology, Parental Choices, and Children's Futures.* New York: Oxford University Press, 2009.

Ruth Deech and Anna Smajdor   *From IVF to Immortality: Controversy in the Era of Reproductive Technology.* New York: Oxford University Press, 2008.

David DeGrazia   *Creation Ethics: Reproduction, Genetics, and Quality of Life.* New York: Oxford University Press, 2012.

David Epstein   *The Sports Gene: Inside the Science of Extraordinary Athletic Performance.* New York: Current, 2013.

Monique Frize   *Ethics for Bioengineers.* San Rafael, CA: Morgan & Claypool, 2012.

Russ Hodge   *Human Genetics: Race, Population, and Disease.* New York: Facts on File, 2010.

Thomas R. Horn and Nita F. Horn — *Forbidden Gates: How Genetics, Robotics, Artificial Intelligence, Synthetic Biology, Nanotechnology, and Human Enhancement Herald the Dawn of Techno-Dimensional Spiritual Warfare.* Crane, MO: Defender, 2011.

Insoo Hyun — *Bioethics and the Future of Stem Cell Research.* Cambridge: Cambridge University Press, 2013.

Isabel Karpin and Kristin Savell — *Perfecting Pregnancy: Law, Disability, and the Future of Reproduction.* Cambridge: Cambridge University Press, 2012.

Robert L. Klitzman — *Am I My Genes?: Confronting Fate and Family Secrets in the Age of Genetic Testing.* New York: Oxford University Press, 2012.

Sheldon Krimsky and Tania Simoncelli — *Genetic Justice: DNA Data Banks, Criminal Investigations, and Civil Liberties.* New York: Columbia University Press, 2010.

Sheldon Krimsky and Kathleen Sloan, eds. — *Race and the Genetic Revolution: Science, Myth, and Culture.* New York: Columbia University Press, 2011.

Sheldon Krimsky and Peter Shorett, eds. — *Rights and Liberties in the Biotech Age: Why We Need a Genetic Bill of Rights.* Lanham, MD: Rowman & Littlefield, 2005.

Ricki Lewis   *Human Genetics: Concepts and Applications.* New York: McGraw-Hill, 2010.

Linda L. McCabe and Edward R. B. McCabe   *DNA: Promise and Peril.* Berkeley: University of California Press, 2008.

Mike McNamee and Verner Møller, eds.   *Doping and Anti-Doping Policy in Sport: Ethical, Legal and Social Perspectives.* New York: Routledge, 2011.

Paul Miller and James Wilsdon, eds.   *Better Humans? The Politics of Human Enhancement and Life Extension.* London: Demos, 2006.

Liza Mundy   *Everything Conceivable: How the Science of Assisted Reproduction Is Changing Our World.* New York: Anchor, 2008.

Luigi Palombi   *Gene Cartels: Biotech Patents in the Age of Free Trade.* Northampton, MA: Edward Elgar, 2009.

Alice Park   *The Stem Cell Hope: How Stem Cell Medicine Can Change Our Lives.* New York: Plume, 2012.

Muireann Quigley, Sarah Chan, and John Harris, eds.   *Stem Cells: New Frontiers in Science and Ethics.* Hackensack, NJ: Scientific, 2012.

Kate Reed   *Gender and Genetics: Sociology of the Prenatal.* New York: Routledge, 2012.

Jose Luis Perez
Trivino

The Challenges of Modern Sport to Ethics: From Doping to Cyborgs. Lanham, MD: Lexington, 2013.

Index